LEAL

LEADING CHANGE

JEZ ROSE

THE LOST ART OF LEADERSHIP

PUBLISHED BY FLATBUSH& BROADWAY
FIRST EDITION PUBLISHED 2024

WRITTEN BY JEZ ROSE
COVER DESIGN BY STEPHEN MAXFIELD
TYPESET IN MERCURE REGULAR & ITALIC

JEZ ROSE is recognized as a leading keynote speaker on the behavioural science of leadership and high performance. Celebrating 21 years at the forefront of positive behaviour change, Microsoft named him as one of the top 10 most sought-after business speakers in North America. Now spending his time between England and the U.S.A., he has worked with most of the Fortune 500 companies to create long-lasting, positive behaviour change with his 'What if?' approach.

A *#1* bestselling author of *Flip the Switch*, *Are You Being Served?*, and a selection of children's books, his celebrated TEDx talks, television work, and YouTube content have garnered over 20 million views. He is the founder of the global self-development platform The Journey.

Watch, listen and follow @ThatJezRose

Contents.

Introduction.

As I write I have now consulted with hundreds of organisations worldwide, and thousands of leaders but I still vividly remember the very first time I was asked for my advice on leadership. I was invited to sit in on a board meeting to see if there might be anything I could suggest which would help them navigate an especially problematic culture the organisation seemed to have found themselves with. It was one of those classic 'friend of a friend' scenarios where someone who knew me and what I was doing happened to be listening to the woes of their friend, the Chief Operating Officer of an international bank. Several weeks later I found myself sat in an extremely plush boardroom which managed to simultaneously be unnecessarily lavish and oppressive, feeling more than a little of a sense of imposter syndrome and wondering how I could ever meet their expectation of adding value.

As soon as the group comprising seven men and one woman began talking, I knew immediately where I could help: language. The words they were using and choosing, were influencing the way they saw themselves and those in their charge but perhaps most importantly were actively shaping the organisation's culture – and not for the better. That meeting started a career advising and problem solving for some of the most recognisable global brands and working with leaders around the world.

Leadership training and the focus on leadership across many sectors, has been way off course for some time now. I'm not entirely sure it was ever focused in the right area. I can't put my finger exactly on the time it started to drift, but I do believe we've been focused, excited - obsessed even - by leadership models, profiling our leaders, and examining frameworks within which leaders can lead. We've spent billions on framework systems that leaders can be guided by for the alleged betterment of the leaders themselves, and subsequently the organisations they work for – the Harvard Business Review suggests it's as much as sixty billion dollars spent annually by global organisations on leadership development programs. From what I've seen, I'm certain a large chunk of that has been a waste. Much has been written about new training pathways for leaders, proffered by expensive global management consultancies and in trust and desperation, signed off by organisations the world over. These have been and continue to be many of my clients. However, after twenty-one years of working with organisations worldwide I've come to realise the future of leadership – and the improvement of our existing leadership - is not in systems, or processes, nor models and frameworks, and that for many years we seem to have been guarding something of an empty safe. All along our focus should have been on the individuals tasked with leading a group of people. The brutal simplicity of leadership is that it is, at its heart, about people leading people and many organisations have overlooked this simple fact. You may be reading this and believe that isn't you or your organisation, which no one would be more delighted to know is true than me, however, I'm going to present to you an argument based on my experience that might suggest otherwise. It is little wonder so many leaders are reporting they are struggling with imposter syndrome*, making the right decisions, or enabling their teams to help them to deliver bigger results, or achieve peak performance, when they simply do not have at their disposal the human tools to lead effectively.

Like many leaders I have met, I want to make the greatest difference I can to my chosen field in the time I have. We are only here once. There is no going back; only the exciting present moment to do something interesting and meaningful with. For many of my clients the measure of a lack of growth or development, let alone mistakes that may set them back, have the potential to be counted in the cost of millions. So, we must stop wallowing in the comfort of five- and ten-year plans and begin choosing the right behaviours to make a difference right now.

During my career to date, I've had the privilege to have taught hundreds of thousands of individuals, from many different groups, cultures, organisations, and backgrounds including elite sports teams, government departments, individuals from stage and screen, and global CEOs. Two of my favourite groups to work with are education professionals, and those in a leadership capacity, especially those already performing at a level others might consider "high performance", or "peak performance". The latter especially because the challenge is greater for me, and I enjoy discovering where else we can take human potential when we believe we have realised its pinnacle. The leaders in both groups tend to spend a lot of time with the individuals in their charge; very often more time than they do with their own families. Both groups are responsible for the nurture and development of others and most have the power or influence to empower, inspire and transform. Equally, however, they have the power to belittle, inhibit, and crush.

At the heart of this book is one core message: truly effective leadership is about people. We must better understand our own behaviour first, to help our teams and organisations – and us – become the best version of ourselves.

I've spent the best part of the last ten years researching the most effective questions to create the greatest difference in the shortest time. This book is peppered with some of those questions, all of which are used by me in my role as advisor to leaders and organisations, and that I've honed and tested in workshops. Think of the questions as activities: stop reading to consider them and see if you're able to readily answer them. To get the most from each, reflect on your answer and explore how you might develop your answer. Think of them as reading breaks; activities to refer back to; inspiration for professional (and no doubt, personal) development, and please do use them in practice with those you lead. I wonder how their responses will differ to yours.

What we do is mirrored in our environment. It has an impact on the outside world. Our responsibility as leaders is significant. It doesn't, however, need to be less human for us to be more effective, despite what may be so commonly role modelled in films, drama, and literature with the austere, domineering, and so often misogynistic character. I care passionately about the way people behave and helping organisations to create fulfilling, results-driven, engaging cultures with long-lasting positive changes to behaviour for everyone.

It is leadership, and leadership alone, which if not creates that environment, supports and maintains it, and it is leadership that I have seen over the last decade, which seems so often to be getting it so very wrong.

It is my wish that this book offers up questions that can be answered, and which help positively influence a different way of approaching the art of leadership - and that it also offers questions that are not so readily answerable, which in turn help us all to reflect more on good practice.

Jez Rose

**According to a KPMG study, 75% of female executives across multiple industries have experienced imposter syndrome. Other studies suggest it is experienced by 71% combined of both genders.*

Foreword by Marshall Goldsmith.

In *Leading Change: The Lost Art of Leadership*, Jez Rose challenges us to rethink our entire understanding of what it means to lead. This is not just another book about management techniques or organizational frameworks; it is a deeply thoughtful exploration into the behaviors, values, and human qualities that form the foundation of authentic leadership.

Jez begins by posing a fundamental question: how often do we confuse "managing" with "leading"? His insight into this distinction is transformative - while management may focus on maintaining systems and processes, true leadership is about inspiring and guiding people toward their best potential.

Drawing from his years of experience as an advisor, behaviorist, and leadership coach to global organizations, Jez unearths the common but often unspoken challenges leaders face. He reveals how many leaders, even at the highest levels, struggle with self-doubt, imposter syndrome, and an overwhelming pressure to meet the often-narrow expectations of corporate roles. Instead of embracing these pressures as inevitable, Jez urges us to view them as opportunities for growth. He argues that effective leadership is less about climbing the corporate ladder and more about nurturing one's own self-awareness and resilience. Only when leaders genuinely understand their own motivations, limitations, and strengths can they create environments where others feel empowered to do the same.

What sets Jez's approach apart is his focus on behavior - both of leaders and their teams. He doesn't simply prescribe a list of rules; instead, he delves into why we behave the way we do, how we can become more self-aware, and how this awareness is critical to leading others. His insights go beyond superficial tactics and aim to cultivate a deeper understanding of human behavior. According to Jez, leadership is not a set of actions but a state of being, a mindset that should influence every interaction. By understanding our own behaviors and motivations, we can better inspire those around us, helping them feel valued, appreciated, and motivated to grow.

Jez's perspective on leadership as a "lost art" is both thought-provoking and timely. In today's fast-paced, outcome-driven world, the softer qualities of leadership - empathy, patience, self-reflection - are often overlooked. Yet Jez reminds us that these qualities are precisely what set apart the leaders we admire. He challenges readers to embrace vulnerability and authenticity, to lead not through authority but through influence and example. This, he argues, is the path to creating truly high performing, engaged teams.

Leading Change is a compelling, practical, and much-needed guide for anyone looking to lead with integrity, authenticity, and purpose. Jez's work is a powerful reminder that the heart of leadership is about people, and that by investing in our own growth and understanding, we can inspire others to do the same.

This book is not just for leaders; it is for anyone committed to making a positive, lasting impact in the lives of others.

Dr. Marshall Goldsmith is the Thinkers50 #1 Executive Coach and New York Times bestselling author of The Earned Life, Triggers, and What Got You Here Won't Get You There.

I

Parallax.

"We don't see things as they are;
we see them as we are."

Anais Nin

I'm sorry if you have the word manager in your job title. I'm sorry because I don't agree with it. When considering leadership, I don't believe the idea of managers should exist. I'm not saying managers aren't useful, but I do believe the concept of management has caused more damage by holding people back and behaving in ways that are unhealthy for workplace cultures, than we may perhaps ever know. If you are a manager, I'm not blaming you personally, but the notion of managers in general. Allow me to explain.

I was asked just yesterday by one of my close friends why I was writing a book about leadership. We've known each other for so long that she probably knows me better than anyone else, and she had a bewildered, almost disappointed look on her face. What she was really dismayed about was not a book about leadership, but that I was writing another book. I've not long finished editing a revised edition of a previous book and am, simultaneously now, writing a book on another topic. My friend knows this means I'll be irritable, and she won't see me as much. But I can't not write this book. Each year I coach ten individuals in senior, or aspiring leadership positions – many of them from brands you'd recognise, some from ones you will have never heard of. In addition, I advise many organisations including most featured in the Fortune 100. I speak at around one hundred conferences a year on leadership and run perhaps twenty or so workshops a year for leaders of all grades. I have been asked by almost every person I coach, and too many times now at events, to write a book about my unique thoughts on leadership, despite there being a seeming ocean of books that exist on the subject. So here we are. I have put it off for many years until I recently discovered, entirely by accident, that I had been doing what I do for twenty-one years. It was a surprise anniversary and prompted much reflection on my achievements, and whether I'd made a difference or had an impact, which for me, is a particularly important part of my work. Has my life so far been meaningful for me, and valuable to others? And what of the next twenty-one years? Why have I spent the past ten years researching the subject of leadership and developing methods based on brain science to help the CEOs and leaders whom I coach, if not to share that information with as many leaders as possible?

That all sounds logical, doesn't it? It certainly played a part in why you're reading this right now, but it wasn't the catalyst. The real trigger was a statistic I read that prompted me to pick up my pencil and begin furiously scribbling notes: everything in my brain on leadership poured out. Advice and guidance I've given; activities I've run; content I've created; questions I've asked and been asked, and the principles of leadership I'd been teaching for the last ten years. What I read was, to me at least, shocking. It's all been because of this:

Seventy nine percent of employees said they have left their organisation because of a lack of appreciation from leaders.

Two thirds of people leave a job because of the leaders they work with. You're reading a book about leadership, so I'm going to assume something about you. It's not just that attrition is directly linked to poor leadership, it's that a huge amount - the majority in fact - of attrition is directly linked to poor leadership.

I wonder where your organisation looks when it has had to deal with attrition. Having acted as an advisor for some of the largest global brands I can confidently say it is not leadership that is put under the microscope first. Or second. Or in my experience indeed for a long time. Leadership teams will, however, put managers under the microscope.

My dismissal of the word manager isn't a twee matter of syntax: I fundamentally believe, along with almost every other psychologist in the world, that the language we use deeply impacts how we think, feel, and behave. In the same way the stories we tell ourselves about our capabilities and worth limit us, or help us to excel, so the concept of being a "manager" has an impact. Several years ago, I began to wonder why it was that leaders, or certainly those with the word leader in their title, so very often behave differently to those labelled a manager. Leadership has a lofty, aspirational air about it, which suggests something more senior, transformational and dare I say a little more important. Like wearing a finely tailored suit, or formal shoes, it changes the way you hold, and feel about, yourself. My method of working is to go back to basics – back to the beginning of the tangled metaphorical ball of string and work out where things began to get messy, then to slowly unravel the tangled middle. As we were dealing with a word that formed part of a job title, I looked up the word manager in the dictionary. What were its origins, I wondered? And there it was. The definition:

Manager. To manage. To cope.

To cope!

I can just imagine all these middle grade managers shouting upstairs to say goodbye to their beloved partners as they leave for work, to be met cheerily with: "have a lovely day, darling!", only for them to turn, solemnly, and respond: "I just hope I cope". It's hardly the most inspiring, or aspiring, way to frame your mind, and it certainly has a significantly different connotation to the word leader, which the dictionary defines as:

Leader. Leadership. The action of leading a group of people or an organisation. The state or position of being a leader.

Leaders get a "state or position"; managers must merely "cope". Immediately, I banished the notion of people thinking of themselves as managers whenever I worked with them; instead thinking about themselves as leaders. This is still met with resistance in the same way it was when I began: people in management roles feel uncomfortable thinking of themselves as leaders. It feels disingenuous to them, as though they are acting above their station, and many report feeling uncomfortable. The power of self-belief is something very few people in my experience sufficiently value or respect. If I tell myself I'm fat, I'll begin to believe it and as a result I'll reach for comforting foods to support my plummeting self-esteem. Those comfort foods are likely high in carbohydrates and fats and just as I imagined, I'll begin to put on weight. I tell myself I'm stupid and I stop trying. Sure enough, other people surpass my ability or intelligence and I become the "stupid" person I imagined myself to be. The secret to great leadership, something I'm asked many, many times, and a topic of discussion with many of the C-suite executives I've advised over the years, is simple: to help other people to want to do something differently. That's it. It may be brutally simple, but there's an awful lot to unpack. The American children's television presenter Fred Rogers, of *Mr. Roger's Neighborhood* fame, cautioned: *"there's a world of difference between insisting on someone's doing something, and establishing an atmosphere in which that person can grow into wanting to do it."* If we can create an environment in which a team of people self-manage, and who remain inspired to do what we need them to do, we can focus entirely on the task of leadership.

Managers do – leaders lead.

The most effective leaders I've worked with in my capacity as an advisor or whilst running workshops, are those who really do embody the notion that leadership is about being a leader. To truly, wholly be something, you must believe it, which is why I believe how you mentally frame yourself is important:

Do you deserve to be a leader?

That's a question only you can answer, but if your innate response is that you're unsure, or don't believe you do, I'd stop reading right now and explore why that is.

Where does that doubt come from?

Even if you are unable to resolve it, it is worth knowing it exists, and that you can help manage it - because it will influence many of your leadership decisions and behaviours, often unknowingly. My work as a behaviourist is to attempt to understand why we do things in the way we do them. In turn, knowing why helps show us how to do things differently – and good leadership is often as much about doing the right things as it is about doing things differently.

If the most efficacious leaders have an inner confidence in their ability to lead – although there is a fine line between confidence and arrogance, and there are plenty of arrogant leaders – where does that inner confidence come from? Is it only achieved through experience and the hard knocks of pin-balling your way up the leadership ladder? Perhaps some people are naturally born leaders and others are merely faking it until they make it? Warren Bennis, the widely regarded pioneer of contemporary leadership studies, was clear on his position of the popular maxim that leaders are born, the leadership equivalent of the nature versus nurture argument: "That's nonsense; in fact, the opposite is true. Leaders are made rather than born." I hear both suppositions regularly with leaders I work closely with. However, this book focuses less on the exhausted and misguided systems, processes, profiling, and the many conflicting principles of leadership, and instead very much on the individual leader and a set of highly effective tools on which they can draw. I'm with Bennis, by the way, and strongly believe great leaders are made, not born. Nurture, not nature, wins this argument. When it comes to behaviour, I'm also firmly in the nurture camp.

If you are uncomfortable by the idea of thinking of yourself as a leader, consider this: if you are responsible for a group of people, you can either be a manager or a leader. The decision as to which word is used is often one of personal preference from whoever came up with job titles where you work. For many I work with, the personal obstacles and challenges to overcome in their role only confirm my position that for too long we have been providing leaders with insufficient and ineffective tools. It needn't be complicated or overly difficult – and it shouldn't be – however, so often we look to external things to help us, instead of doing the work ourselves. As Aesop warned: "Beware lest you lose the substance by grasping at the shadow." Am I saying that managers should consider themselves as leaders? Yes. Am I suggesting there is therefore no place for managers? Perhaps. What are "managers" anyway? If people leading people is leadership, perhaps it is time to consider quite what we mean by "manager", if nothing more than a lesser paid leader.

This begins with changing our view of what is possible and firmly within our ability to influence. As a species we are experts at focusing far too much on the reasons for our failures, and not nearly enough on the causes of our success – it's almost habit that we replay where we went wrong in minute detail, criticising, and critiquing. Yet our achievements are celebrated and assessed fleetingly, if at all, before we refocus on the next. Behaviour in itself is habitual; effective leadership means creating strong, beneficial habits not only for leaders, but for those in our charge. Having spent almost ten years researching the most effective, efficient, and quickest ways to change behaviours, I believe this process begins with asking more questions: leaders must ask questions of themselves and of those they lead, and they should ask way more than my experience shows they currently do. Questions cause a pattern interrupt: an unexpected interruption that breaks the regular patterns of our brain's processing and flow, in turn helping to alter our mental, emotional, or behavioural state. Some pattern interrupts feel like those mildly confusing moments when you can't think of the word; others are like having the rug pulled from under your feet, and yet others feel like a scream ripping through a dinner party. These interruptions to our constant, subconscious behaviours and decisions force us to momentarily stop what we're doing; pause and reflect as we seek the answer – and those two things are the lifeblood of effective leadership. It's in that magical moment of pause and reflection that we can potentially choose an alternative, more positive outcome. Questions serve as brilliant pattern interrupts: they stimulate our brain to stop what it was doing and search for an answer to the challenge presented in the question. If we can't readily supply an answer, the questions force our brain to reflect and consider what the answer may be. They are free, effective, portable, and one of my favourite leadership tools. Exactly what questions to ask, though? That's a good question! In fact, if you're ever unsure of what question to ask, this is the perfect place to start:

What is the right question to ask right now?

If we stop asking questions, or don't ask enough of them, we hold ourselves back, and as we shall explore further, we have a core responsibility to those in our charge to encourage development. Just one simple question can help change everything. In many cases the question will do all the heavy lifting, saving hours of angst and worry. The questions I'll share with you in this book have been used to help teachers and education professionals better manage challenging behaviour in the classroom; to resolve problems at C-suite level; rid silo working behaviours; realign cultural connections; ignite creativity and manage and resolve many classic leadership challenges. A question isn't always the right response, but I find that if nothing else it helps buy everyone some time by pressing pause on thinking and behaviours, providing you opportunity to reflect and choose the most appropriate response. The question doesn't always provide a direct answer, although that is often down to the nature of how the question is constructed, however, they almost always prompt discussion, thinking, and reflection. Often that vicarious creative process can result in a greater benefit than a definitive answer by generating creative solutions, or indeed the alignment on the importance to not decide right now but instead seek further information. I'm reminded of Lord Byron's question that, while rhetorical, provides an important pattern interrupt when reflecting on pain or trauma caused by negative actions: "What deep wounds ever closed without a scar?".

The onus is not always on leaders to provide answers for the questions we pose; it can be especially useful and effective to allow our team to provide answers. A common misconception I hear time and again is that leaders should have all the answers to all the questions – I would caution anyone who believes that to be the case. Leaders are not supposed to have all the answers at all – that mentality is sailing close to dictatorship. A golden thread running throughout effective leadership is empowerment, and one of the simplest ways to empower those in your charge, whilst simultaneously cultivating a unified culture of solution-orientated thinking, is to ask:

What do you think is the right decision to make for us as a team, right now?

Look at those in your charge not as a separate entity, but as an extension of your leadership counsel. If your decisions and actions impact them, should they not at least be partly involved in those decisions?

Marshall Goldsmith, the multi-award-winning leadership coach whom I feel honoured to know, was named twice by Thinkers 50 as the "number one leadership thinker in the world". He is the New York Times bestselling author of, among several other books, *What Got You Here Won't Get You There.* Marshall kindly wrote a positive review for my first number one bestselling book, *Flip the Switch.* I've admired his kindness and generosity for many years and despite being in great demand, he graciously agreed to be interviewed as part of my research for this book. I asked him who the individuals were in his life that really stood out as examples of great leaders, whom also had the greatest impact on him and his own leadership style.

In true Marshall style, his first response was to praise one of his friends, a leader who has had an impact on Marshall's own thoughts about leading people. Alan Mulally was the CEO of Ford Motor Company from 2006 to 2014, and under his leadership the company's stock value rocketed from $1.01 to $18.40. Alan has known Marshall now for thirty-eight years, since when he first asked Marshall to be his leadership coach. However, the most insightful lesson from Marshall's time with Alan is possibly not what you might imagine. Marshall realised when analysing the time spent with his clients, that his most successful clients spent the least amount of time with him; indeed, there was a truly negative correlation to the improvement of a client and the time spent being coached by Marshall. Curious, he asked Alan what it was that he had learnt about coaching during their sessions together, and the response was not about technicality, or a specific strategy or technique, but, as Marshall said: "coaching is all about client selection; you pick the right customer, and you win – pick the wrong customer and you lose. While CEO of Ford, Alan said he didn't design the cars; he didn't make the cars; he didn't build the cars. 'It's not about me – it's about them'. Marshall continued: "one of the smartest things he did was to frequently answer questions with questions. He would respond by asking if anyone else in Ford was better placed to answer the question that had been asked of him as CEO, or if they should hire someone to better answer the question than him. It's very smart thinking and so few leaders ever get this. The great myth is that if someone understands something, they will do it. If they read a book on leadership, they will understand it but doing it is hard because you must do it all by yourself."

I hope to build a strong enough case for scrapping the title "manager", in turn creating great cultural change in your organisation by encouraging you to vicariously develop a new generation of leaders with job titles that positively influence their thinking and behaviour. Titles that set people up to lean into it and behave as their title encourages them to. The approach to behaviour change I have adopted came about by both a personal appreciation for efficiency, but also a need for rapid efficacy. By the time I become involved, many of my clients are being scrutinised and need to demonstrate results to senior leaders, stakeholders, or indeed governing bodies, as quickly as possible. Rather than implementing one change or recommending one specific strategic adjustment and waiting to assess efficacy, I simultaneously opt for the five or so I believe will be the most efficacious: a multi-pronged approach. I encourage all leaders I work with to carry a metaphorical tool belt containing as many highly effective questions, behaviour change strategies, and problem-solving tactics as will hypothetically fit in it, as possible. At least some of those should be ways to encourage existing behaviours to continue, otherwise known as behavioural nudges. This way leadership becomes more hands-off, or self-managing, for the individuals in their charge. One of those tools is considering ways to positively alter how our team thinks and feels about, and believes in, themselves. Their title is a great place to start. There's a big difference in the emotional impact of being a "Media Master" compared to introducing yourself as a "Social Media Manager". The same for "Number Ninja", as opposed to an "Accountant". The titles don't need to be twee, or comical as they are here, they simply need to avoid the idea that they manage - or cope – and instead inspire.

Here are two deceptively simple questions to answer before we continue. By the time you finish this book you may want to amend your answers, but attempt to consider what your response would be right now:

What makes you a good leader?

Why do you lead?

At this stage of our journey together there really are no correct, or incorrect, answers; only what feels honest and true to you right now. Naturally, there's no need to share your answers with anyone, and so I'd encourage you to look inwardly and answer truthfully to yourself. Previous answers to the first question from leaders I have coached include: "I'm good at getting results from other people"; "my CV", and "my team has the lowest attrition rate of our entire organisation". To the second question responses have included: "for the money"; "being a leader makes me feel important", and "because it is expected of me". If this journey we are about to embark on is going to work at all you must first identify where you are starting from so you're able to successfully move from where you are to where you want to be – or indeed, where you could be.

If you believe you're a manager, you're going in the wrong direction.

2
Do, or Lead.

"People buy into the leader before they buy into the vision."

John Maxwell

One of my newest coaching clients is the Director of Human Resources for an international Fintech company. This week during our scheduled call Rachel raised an issue she was having with her Group Managing Director, in particular his compulsion to be actively involved in every detail of the decisions she is making. As if the micro-managing wasn't distracting and oppressive enough, the additional stress he was putting himself under by being involved in everyone's decision making process was creating an especially stressful environment for everyone else. To add fuel to the fire, there were questions being asked with increasing frequency by the board about commercial direction and the lack of reporting. What Rachel had come to realise, unfortunately this way, was that the Group MD was spending too much time doing, and not nearly enough leading. If we build teams who can self-manage, we are able to confidently focus on leading.

The difference between great leadership and managing people - whether you're a manager or a leader by title - is largely mindset. I define the 'doing' things in leadership as micro-managing and firefighting: metaphorically (or literally!) rolling your sleeves up and physically getting, or being, involved. Of course, it's important for me to generalise here because this book is not focused on one field of specialty, or industry sector – in some cases it may be essential for leaders to be actively involved in doing things, however, I'd caution that in most cases. I've come to know it should be the exception not the rule, and even then, only temporarily when essential. While we are involved in a task it is impossible to have an effective, simultaneous wider focus: attempting to lead whilst micromanaging makes for less effective leadership (and is incredibly irritating for others involved). Perhaps the best example of a clearly definitive difference in doing and leading can be seen in emergency medicine. If you are ever unfortunate enough to be in a resuscitation bed in a hospital emergency department, you will observe several nurses, healthcare assistants, and specialty doctors tending to you. Most of those have only one role, whether that be obtaining intravenous access, monitoring the patient's physiological signs, examining changes in their condition, or assessing and treating injuries. They are working in silos: individuals with specialist knowledge focused on their specific task and trusting others to deliver on theirs. Those with a subject specialty will be in attendance for their specialist knowledge of the sole area or process of the body. At the foot end of the bed, occasionally on a small box to raise their sightline, will be stood an emergency consultant: the clinical lead. They have total clinical oversight and responsibility for the patient, their treatment, and care. They are the "team leader" by title and design, and an important part of their role is to remain hands-off unless necessary. From their hands-off vantage point, they must learn to trust; sometimes guiding, and suggesting to those in their charge to carry out specific observations, tests, and interventions that provide them with information they need to make overall decisions about the patient's care. At any given point when new information is available, perhaps because of a change in the patient's condition, their plan and instructions may change – often rapidly. Emergency department consultants are a great visual reminder of how efficacious leadership should look: trusting teams to fulfil their role to the best of their ability; occasionally reminding, guiding, or encouraging, but ultimately leading - not doing.

And yet in the little over ten years I have been coaching leadership executives, it is perhaps the most common difficulty my client's recount. The problem is not in their teams working in silos, nor in an overwhelming desire to micro-manage. Nor is it often an issue with the individual's personality. The core issue preventing us from confidently leading is a lack of trust and self-confidence. Most have not spent sufficient time developing a culture of trust, honesty, and positive communication and just as many I meet lack confidence in their ability or knowledge as leaders. The latter more personal issue is to blame for the passive aggressive micromanaging and inability to relinquish control for fear of something going wrong and being put under the microscope, lest people discover they're merely a sheep in wolf's clothing.

When invited to assist a leadership cohort that is in trouble, I find very often that the symptoms are often the same. Usually, these groups of people form a leadership team because they have demonstrated the aptitude and experience required by the organisation to lead pockets of the organisation. Not always, but sometimes, those people will be described to me by senior executives requesting my assistance as "disengaged with their leadership responsibilities", "overworked", "under pressure", or "working in silos". I keep notes from every call I have with clients and at the beginning of each new year, review my notes from the previous. In those notebooks stretching back almost fifteen years I look for patterns, themes, and commonalities across industry sectors, and changes over time. The story presented to me is often remarkably similar. It may well be a different industry or organisation, but it's largely the same people problem. The solution is most often not merely additional leadership training. There are almost always other, deeper factors influencing behaviour, including issues with culture, trust, confidence in autonomy, and inherited feedback challenges which result in whole swathes of the organisation operating without productive communication channels. There is, however, one element which is almost always present: leaders being too involved. When a leader tells me they don't have time to lead, it raises a red flag telling of several things about them: primarily that they are *doing* too much, and not *leading* enough.

Who in your team can you trust to do a little more than they are tasked with currently?

Who requires additional training or support so you're able to do less for them?

What support is available to you as a leader, which you don't necessarily see as your support? For example, are there training opportunities for your team; learning partner programs – or opportunities to create them – or an under-developed trust with those in your charge?

Sometimes all people need is encouragement, and the support to make mistakes enabling them to learn and thrive through curiosity. We often expect far too much from those around us though and expect their thought process and output to be the same as ours - with the information we are privy to but which they may not be. In response, people become fearful of making mistakes and begin working within tightly defined safe comfort zones which stifle risk, creativity, development – and trust. The quickest and most effective way to grow your team's confidence is through trust, however, deep trust is accumulated over time, and nothing can replace that necessary repetition of rupture and repair for us to see and learn enough times that the trust is consistent and reliable. Trust is like a plugged sink, which begins empty but with every comfortable response or behaviour exhibited, a small amount of water is added, incrementally. A cross word, unpredictable or contradictory response and the plug is momentarily removed depleting the trust level. If the trust is not immediately regained, the plug remains out and the trust rapidly drains away. There's no fast track to gaining trust; it is both won, or lost, gradually and just like establishing savings, or clearing debt, everyone must put effort into slowly getting closer to the target of a full sink. I encourage all leaders I work with to make it a priority focus, not only for their own benefit but for those they lead. Preserving and demonstrating trust is everyone's responsibility. The act of earning it creates an especially positive cultural shift on which to build a strong and effective team with more predictable, beneficial, and positive behaviours. In this respect there's a combination of doing and leading because effective leadership is as much about showing up and contributing to the culture as it is about leading it.

When I interviewed Marshall Goldsmith about influential and inspirational leaders he had worked with, he had an interesting point to reflect on: "The thing about Frances, and Alan - I never, after hundreds of hours in their company, heard either of them complain about anything. If you're in a leadership role, it's 'show time'. There's no time for "poor me"; "my headache hurts", or for it to be about you - and that's not being a phony. In my book that's being a professional. Leadership isn't about focusing on what you need; it's about focusing on what they need."

I appreciate it can feel worrying to let go of the doing when low trust levels exist. If you're concerned about letting go and empowering your team to do more, take a moment to first examine how you honestly feel about trust. You might find it useful to confidentially highlight the areas where trust is an issue for you, and to reflect on how those might be repaired, perhaps by starting with small, low-risk tasks to help build trust through results. When reflecting on trust make sure to not excuse lack of experience or cultural issues such as silo working as solely issues with trust. If your team have not been empowered or encouraged to act confidently and without retribution these are perhaps issues primarily with their trust of you, or the organisation. Often, we behave in a way, or assume a mindset, because of our interpretation of behaviour deflected by others. A critical element of effective leadership is first seeking to understand the reality of a situation, not simply the perception on face value. That can sometimes feel a little like detective work, but far too many leaders act reactively, and not responsively, only fuelling the deterioration of trust.

From conversations I've had with the teams of my leadership clients, it is true to say that many people assume leadership is a position bestowed on those who are already good at it, or want it, not a skill learned, honed, and finessed over many years. The reality is often completely the opposite, of course because leadership is a craft. Whereas 'leader' is merely a title no different to missus, or Lord. Research would suggest many leaders do not think about leadership seriously enough or spend sufficient time developing their skills in it: only forty-eight percent of employees view their company's leadership as high quality with one in two admitting they've left a job to escape from a bad manager.

Our ability as a species to ably adapt and evolve benefits us in many ways. It continues to inspire and astound me just how quickly we can change if we want or need to. Prior to the global Covid-19 pandemic the concept of working from home was alien to most of my clients. Traditional holiday requests were the only way one could secure time away from the office unless an offsite meeting promised a change of scenery. You may remember during this time in 2019, one of the topical corporate buzz words was "agile". Agile working, agile modelling, agile sales – everyone was so confident they were agile, if not lean, too. Overnight the associated pandemic lockdowns evidenced that organisations didn't have sufficient laptops or systems to support working from home, and the subsequent delays to provide the infrastructure required demonstrated how very few truly were agile. We like to believe we are in full control, and indeed possess or at least have access to, the answers we may need; it boosts our confidence and innate desire for validation. In practice, however, our weaknesses are exposed if we don't ask sufficient questions. The seeking of further information through questioning prompts creativity and opportunity, and an essential leadership skill is knowing which questions to ask, which I will cover in more detail. The questions we should have asked when we were busy feeling smug about being lean and agile were more "what if?" questions, with wild and crazy hypothesis, followed up by: "how do we resolve this?". Clearly no one could have anticipated the devastation and chaos Covid-19 brought with it, however, many could have been much better prepared. It is the responsibility of leaders to identify weaknesses and act on them. On that alone, many failed to demonstrate they were the leaders they imagined they were.

3
A Very Particular Set of Skills.

"Imagination is more important than knowledge."

Albert Einstein

I have always been drawn to seek a better understanding of why it is that humans can be both so savage and luminous toward one another – the difference in behaviours exhibited toward our fellow human can be striking.

In the last eighteen months my office has seen a significant increase in enquiries about leadership coaching, and my leadership workshops. If this book was out already, I could put it down to that, but it isn't. However, a piece of data was released that possibly helps to explain what's going on and why there appears to be a sudden increase in focus on leadership development. As of 2022, eighty three percent of organisations responded to a survey confirming they believe it's important to develop leaders at all levels in a company. That's quite the shift from ten years ago when I only really worked with senior executives and C-suite members, where much of the focus was on professional career development rather than progressing the individual, per-se. However, and here's the linchpin, only five percent who responded in that piece of research implement the improvements identified when working to improve leadership. Perhaps more worrying is the latest research published by Forbes, which states that sixty percent of CEOs believe they don't have high quality leaders in their team. My first thought was: how did it get to that point? Perhaps this is the reason why poor leadership statistics are so much more common than statistics about good leadership - the leadership landscape is worse than many knew it to be. I'd like to change that, which is why I'm sat writing about why great leadership is so important whilst in Heathrow Airport, waiting to fly to work with a client in Scotland having just come from speaking at a company conference in Ibiza.

I have asked probably tens of thousands of people, over the past ten years a simple question: "did you receive any training for your leadership role?". As you might imagine almost everyone answers affirmatively. I then ask if at some point following their leadership training they have purchased a book about management or leadership, such as the iconic *Who Moved My Cheese?* or *One Minute Manager*. The majority confirm they have indeed bought further books on leadership, which exposes one interesting revelation: that their leadership training did not provide them with all the skills, or answers, they required. Following their training they went, probably semi-confidently, into the workplace and were left lacking. They wanted more. They needed more. They needed answers. And so, they reached for a book. We have entire leadership cohorts largely making it up as they go along, and that's not only unfair on them and those in their charge, but it's also unnecessary. The leadership arena is awash with agendas, models, frameworks, and systems that allegedly tell us how to lead, and it can be difficult to know where to turn. My approach has always been to keep things as simple as possible - efficacious, but simple. I have nothing to prove to anyone, nor do I need to unnecessarily over-complicate things to be validated. When it comes to leadership there's really no need to over complicate it: it's about people. Unnecessarily complicating things does not make us look more intelligent, or indeed make us better leaders, as both Alan Mullaly and Frances Hesselbein brilliantly demonstrated by their own examples.

Newly appointed leaders require a particular set of skills to principally encourage and support growth and confidence in the individual, helping them achieve the results required of them in a fresh role, which can often be daunting. However, experienced leaders require a different set of skills to efficaciously manage the behaviour, mindset, and output of those in their charge. There are a common set of behavioural skills, which overlap these two different points in career, which interestingly are almost always observed in high performing leaders. They help see what the competition can't, and efficiently motivate and inspire those in their charge to want to change or do something differently. Unfortunately, leadership isn't only about positively encouraging and inspiring; it's equally about resolving people problems. Almost all leadership problems - and by that, I mean the challenges most leaders are faced with when it comes to those in their charge - are behavioural, and mindset plays a key role in not only forming but reinforcing our behaviours. So often I listen to a CEO frustratedly bemoan they can't change a behaviour when they've not even considered mindset. Now, the internet is awash with opinions on what the core leadership skills are, and the essential characteristics of good leaders. Much is simply recycled, but when we shift our attention from leadership as a structure, and consider the individual leader on a human level, there are skills I believe important for every leader. They aren't exhaustive, but they are the ones I'll be focusing most on within this book, and I'll explain why.

As leaders, we must become better at asking questions of ourselves, and of the people in our charge, and of every situation we find ourselves in. Like much of the species, we are at fault of accepting too much on face value or acting without asking important questions that help better shape our behaviours, decisions, and consequences. Most of us go through life with a firmly established set of beliefs formed in childhood and through formative developmental periods. The questions we must ask as leaders form what I refer to, rather unimaginatively, as a Leadership Toolbox: essential elements, or tools, that help us become more effective leaders by challenging established or precondition beliefs and frameworks.

The questions are most effective when we consider them ourselves first and try to form an answer. You may be unable to provide a concrete or fully formed answer on your own, but that doesn't matter because the second part of this exercise is to put the same questions to your team – those in your charge. Each creates a powerful discussion point and an effective exercise in bringing your team closer together by clearly defining the values on which they act as a team.

The first question is the deceptively simple:

Who are we?

It's important to ask and define this question first because it deals with identity: as a leader, and as a team, who are you? Only when you know who you are, can you ask the second question:

What are we doing?

You must know who you are before you begin to define more clearly what your purpose is as a leader, and as a team. Really spend time to be clear about the detail here. Only then when you know who you are and what you are doing can you ask the third question:

What are we doing?

What better question to answer to help with clarity? It's a question that is more challenging to answer than it first appears. Finally, only when you know who you are, what you are doing, and why you are doing it can you ask the fourth question:

How do we make it better?

This final question, for me, is important because it forces us to consider integrity – and integrity is a key leadership quality I'll discuss further. Four simple questions that provide useful food for thought and reflection, but also move you and your team forwards, together. There are many more questions throughout this book. Asking the right questions leads us to new areas, whilst first causing us to pause, effectively acting as what psychologists call a pattern interrupt. Our brains are continually processing information at a speed and level we are consciously unaware of. Right now, your brain is converting these shapes into letters, into words, and into meaning. It is simultaneously cross-matching that with existing information or knowledge it might match to, whilst assessing the temperature, the comfort of your entire body, your hunger, thirst, and energy levels – and on and on. Much of our decisions, behaviours and what we say are largely unconsidered; for much of our life we are on autopilot. Pattern interrupts are stimuli that stop us in our tracks, forcing us to reassess. For example, if when walking out of the supermarket with your shopping bags, someone approached you and said: "it's not the 29th of March!", your brain is sent into a mad search for information, immediately interrupting the flow of regular patterns, like searching for the familiar route back to the car, listening for moving cars, assessing the weight and comfort of the shopping bags etc. Your brain now has random, new information to consider: Who is this person? Do I know them? What is today's date? What happened on March 29th? Why is the date relevant? Where is my pepper spray? This is a pattern interrupt. The best interrupts are questions: they cause us to pause, reflect, and consider an answer to the question. The more questions of the type that are useful and effective you have as a leader, the more confident, and more effective a leader you'll be. You may well think of your own questions, prompted as we together journey through this book. I'd encourage you to collect and write them somewhere you can easily reference them. I've intentionally included a few blank pages at the rear of the book for just that, so if you've a pen handy you can jot them there.

On leading language.

While considering the subject of language, interestingly the phrases 'I love you', and 'I hate you', have the same number of words, and letters – and incidentally the same Scrabble score (fourteen if you're wondering). However, what distinguishes them from each other is an entirely different emotional resonance the words have when they are spoken and heard. The language we choose to use as leaders can belittle, crush, and disengage our team, or empower, unite, and inspire them. Our languages are simply noises made in our throat, and yet depending on how you understand and interpret those noises, you know what my intention, needs, or desires are. The problem, best explained I think by trying to speak to someone from another country who doesn't speak your language, is speaking slowly and raising your voice. I once witnessed someone do this to a visually impaired person – such is the total lack of understanding of disabilities among our fellow species. Our reasoning is that if we repeat the same thing, but slower and louder, they will understand. Leaders are often guilty of this: we run with the leadership style we are comfortable with, neglecting to consider the language, comprehension and learning needs of others and how our style must be readily adaptable for those. In 2020, the United Kingdom's Cabinet Office Behavioural Insights Team published the results of one of their many successful and interesting trials. While nine out of ten people support organ donation, only one in three in the U.K. are registered, and with three people dying every day due to a lack of available organs, the NHS Blood and Transplant service understandably needed to increase the number of donors. Through simply changing the wording on an online form, they increased the number of sign-ups. In fact, so impressive were the results that the research team calculated if the best performing message was used over an entire year, compared to the trial period, it would result in an additional ninety-six thousand donor registrations. The language we use is powerful, and worth our careful consideration - particularly so in leadership. Even the simplest of words can have significant consequences. For example, tell a child they can't do something, and they give up; they simply learn to not try. The word 'can't' can be equally destructive for adults for the same reason. However, it isn't only about the specific words used, but is as much about the context in which they are used, and the impact words can have when used correctly. When working in England's National Health Service (NHS) I was supervised by a manager who was, to quote them: "busier than you could ever imagine". Emails sent to them were returned with single word responses, either "yes", or "no". You knew when they were especially busy – presumably even busier than the busiest that I could ever imagine – because the responses became single letters: "y", or "n". I have always quite enjoyed being the cat among the pigeons, to help encourage different ways of doing things and thinking, especially when it comes to things that don't sit right with me. Martin Luther King famously declared during a sermon in Selma, Alabama in 1965:

"A man dies when he refuses to stand up for that which is right. A man dies when he refuses to stand up for justice. A man dies when he refuses to take a stand for that which is true."

And so, I began writing longer and longer emails to my manager, which eventually became lengthy enquiries and responses, multiple paragraphs in length, until one day they snapped. The telephone on my desk rang and as I answered I was met by the irate tones of my manager demanding to know why I was wasting their time, and mine, with such unnecessarily lengthy emails, which they did not have the time to read. I carefully explained that this was the most they had spoken to me in almost six months, how grateful I was for their time, and how valued I felt because of it. They continued with the reprimand and their telephone was slammed down. I replaced the receiver and three days later received an email from my manager, which was two sentences long. Progress. Cat, one – pigeons, nil.

Part of my role when working with leadership teams, whether in an advisory, coach, or trainer capacity, is to help review best practice. I may offer alternative behaviours or ways of thinking that may be more efficacious or to inspire confidence in the individual's ability as a leader. One of the tools I find most useful, which has wide ranging impact, is to encourage changing annual performance reviews to quarterly reviews. The most common excuse I am offered as to why this isn't possible is that there isn't sufficient time to conduct the annual reviews, which in themselves cause significant additional workloads and stress, so there is no way that quadrupling that workload would be possible. However, annual reviews are ineffective for several reasons, not least because by their very nature you are saving eleven months of feedback up to unpack, review, and make action plans for, in just one annual meeting. It seems ludicrous to me that any leader would be formally out of touch with those in their charge for such long periods. Undertaking quarterly reviews encourages a culture of binary feedback. It keeps leaders in touch with their teams, and very quickly, within perhaps two or three sessions, transitions to brief conversations in corridors. The overly processed meeting with associated paperwork and action plans gives way to a much more fluid and dynamic way of asking for and receiving feedback where leaders are much more in touch with the everyday tone of those they lead. I am pleasantly surprised when I speak to groups of middle or senior grade leaders who conduct monthly reviews because it helps to evidence how normal and simple this method of communication is. I've no idea why the idea of annual reviews has stuck around for so long, becoming the unchallenged de-rigour, but I'm pleased that others are also beginning to ask: "why do we do it this way?", and "how do we make it better?". Who leaders are, how they should behave and what leadership is has been largely unchallenged, and I believe this has led to more leaders feeling insecure and the data which shows how ineffective leadership is. We don't need radical changes to leadership or management strategies, or to recruit in futuristic ways, or incorporate artificial intelligence into our candidate selection. We simply need to focus more on the people and encourage leaders to ask more questions.

By asking more questions we get to explore alternative ways of thinking and behaving. For example:

"What happens in your job that makes you want to quit?"

A question that's worth asking yourself every now and again, but it's a critical question to ask your team. You really need to know the answer now, not in six months, or two years-time when it's too late and their unwavering resignation lands on your desk. Or indeed when something becomes unmanageable for you anymore, and you find yourself unhappy and looking to get out. Yet another benefit of those quarterly reviews: an opportunity to ask more questions. My consistently curious mind asks a lot of questions, a lot of the time. Occasionally there is silence in my mind, but very rarely. In 2019 I was involved in a piece of research conducted by the Coca Cola company as part of a new product launch in the U.K., which resulted in a remarkable and chillingly insightful piece of data: ninety seven percent of people in London did not notice nature on their daily commute. Initially I found this staggering and was convinced there was an error in the research. In a major city where trees outnumber people, how could only three percent be aware of nature when commuting to work? Was tiredness to blame? Had we asked people travelling during dark mornings? I sat on a train on the way back home from London, looking out of the window at a beautiful sunset and as I turned to look around the packed carriage, not a single other passenger had noticed the arresting rays of that setting sun. They all, without exception, sat looking at a mobile phone, tablet, computer, book, or newspaper. At that moment I knew the data was right, and I was overcome with dread at what this meant for our future.

On getting used to things.
The heady, all-consuming feeling of falling in love is like no other. We will do anything to please and appease new lovers. Our own boundaries are often compromised, and our life patterns flexed to help demonstrate our affection: early morning rises to gently creep out of bed and make a surprise cup of coffee

for them; the writing of little notes tucked into coat pockets to be discovered later at work; random gift purchases; the cancelling of plans to make a surprise visit; late night discussions that extend way after your normal bedtime rituals. All these behaviours and more to show the other how serious you are about your declaration of love – or lust. Fast forward perhaps six months; perhaps you're now living together. Or five years and you're now married. What is left of those rituals? Think of your current, or most recent relationship and the courting rituals you undertook in that initial period of intense lust, compared to how time gently erodes the acts, slowly reducing in number and frequency. Does time erode our desire? Perhaps. However, what we are concerned with here is how strikingly adaptive we are, and how quickly we habituate. Habituation essentially means "getting used to" and is an incredibly important part of our psychology allowing us to adapt and evolve to differing circumstances and environments. Compare how exposed, lost, and overwhelmed you felt on your first day at work, flooded by trying to navigate systems, processes and physical environments: Which button am I supposed to press now? Where are the toilets? Which one is Alan? Compare that to how you feel about those same things six months on when everything feels so much more familiar. Habituation helps us cope with things that change around us, and some people are much better at adapting – or habituating – than others. However, habituation can also be our greatest barrier for growth. It is because we habituate that our once love-filled relationships grow stale, and why the cute notes stop, and the energy ends. We get used to that person being a part of our lives; being there when we come home. The routines become predictable and in turn we appreciate them less. And so it is at work, which is often why so much resistance is felt when significant changes are made to operating procedures, or models of working: they threaten what we know to be right and true, and real.

A friend of my mother's moved with her two young children to a house that had in its garden a giant horse chestnut tree. Every year in spring, the tree would begin to shed its giant glossy brown seeds, which in Britain we call conkers, wrapped in the green spikey casing. The smooth, glossy seed has been for at least one hundred years used as the centre piece of a game with the same name: conkers. Through the centre of the seed a small hole is drilled, and a length of string threaded, then secured with a knot against one edge of the conker. Holding tightly the end of the string furthest from the conker, letting the seed dangle down, the objective is to swing it directly at an opponent's conker until one is destroyed. The person with the conker remaining most intact, or still on the string, is declared the winner. My mother's friend's two boys were ecstatic about the conker tree in their new garden and couldn't wait to play. That first year, conkers were frozen, pickled, and stored in darkness to discover how to create a strong, reliable, winning conker. A tournament took place and late into the summer and autumn evenings that first year the boys played under their newly acquired tree. The following year, however, it was reported that the boys had not really bothered much with conkers. They had habituated to the conker tree in the same way we habituate to our loved ones; our relationships; our income; colleagues; opportunities; health – to life.

On the sum of the whole.

I have written much about my use of the 'stacking' technique, but mostly in practical terms within the context of customer service. However, it is behavioural in its method, which is precisely why it is successfully used in retail sales. A retailer will place our purchase in an especially nice bag, with rope handles, for example. However, the item you've purchased is first wrapped in tissue paper, sprayed with an evocative scent and everything sealed with a branded sticker. Stacking works because the sum of the whole is greater than the individual parts, and that's a concept we should be encouraging as leaders. I want to help create teams who self-manage, self-regulate and who readily offer suggestions for improvements, no matter how small or insignificant they believe they are. This part is key. Creativity that encourages input should always be encouraged. The result of a member of your team suggesting something benign, such as moving the printer closer to their desks to reduce the time spent travelling to it, encourages others to suggest small but useful and practical improvements, too. Gradually the sum of the whole becomes greater than the individual parts, with a team who become solution-orientated and readily monitor and manage their own environment, workload and working behaviours for further improvements. On occasion when I suggest employing principles like stacking, or during discussions or workshops with leaders, individuals will tell me they don't have time to employ new or different techniques that will ultimately help drive change or improve their teams. Those individuals are almost always suffering with change fatigue or overwhelmed with workload and organisational pressures. Regardless, "I don't have enough time to be a good leader" is a red flag.

I hear variations on that theme from leaders including the worse: "I don't have time to lead". Who are the promising leaders you can delegate to and develop, to simultaneously help you with your workload and subsequently help empower on their own leadership development journey? When we utilise those individuals in a win-win situation that helps embolden their own growth journey, it helps manage our own workload - and time - in a remarkably efficient way to great effect. Equally, what are you doing about those not performing well to help get them back on track? Those individuals can also be tasked with projects, or to assist with your task list. This is one of my favourite strategies to employ. By virtue of them being entrusted with only a part of a project, they are obliged to maintain contact with you, providing you with an ideal opportunity, self-managed by them, to ensure their performance is positively encouraged and improved. Once we've looked at the people around us, we can turn our attention to changes that need making to systems and processes, which can help improve performance and engagement: key performance indicators, even if local or individual; changes to recruitment criteria; quarterly reviews and what is discussed during them; communication etc. Often the cause or trigger of the problematic behaviour is in other areas such as these.

When a captain takes legal and official charge of the aircraft they are flying, their mental and physical check list includes the aircraft itself; the crew; their own ability; overall safety; passenger compliance and safety; navigation; overall leadership – it's more than simply flying the plane. Thankfully, all the captains I've met and been flown by understand this. Imagine if the captain decided to ignore some of those other elements because they felt they were too busy or felt they didn't have enough time to lead. They boarded, shut the door, looked straight ahead, and flew the plane, all the while oblivious to communication, navigation, passenger needs or developing situations with the aircraft. As ludicrous as this scenario sounds, it is exactly what happens in organisations across the world when leaders neglect the wider elements of their role as a leader by saying they don't have time. The feeling of having insufficient time is a genuine, real, and frustrating issue, and I know it causes problems and restricts workflow. However, there are many additional elements, many more moving parts to being an effective leader more complex than justifying away our business. When we are more aware of those, we are better equipped to lead more effectively.

4
Leopard Spots.

"What people have the capacity to choose,
they have the ability to change."

Madeleine Albright

'A leopard cannot change its spots' is a phrase that frustrates me. It doesn't really make sense. The spots on a leopard are a permanent part of evolutionary biology. They are genetic and a part of its very DNA. The only way a leopard would change its spots would be through a long process of selective breeding of which it wouldn't have any control. However, behaviour is not solely controlled by our DNA like a leopard's spots: it is modelled and learnt. Environment and modelling are the greatest influences on shaping our behaviours, although, some genetics do influence how our behaviours present, for example, in psychological disorders. To talk about someone's lack of change in their behaviour by comparing them to a leopard's inability to adapt its appearance is not accurate, and negatively influences how we approach not only the problem facing us, but the individual concerned. Beginning any challenge with an open mind is always going to lead us to a better solution and make the journey to it much less frustrating or problematic.

Do you remember a leader from an existing or previous employment – or perhaps even a schoolteacher – who you particularly admired?

What was it about them that you respected or admired? Specifically what characteristics or values made such an impression on you?

These recollections make for useful benchmarks to which we

can aspire and be mindful of when making our own decisions as a leader about our mindset and the decisions we make.

What would [your memorable leader] do?

What would they say?

What would they think about this?

These are powerful and useful questions to keep coming back to, which help us feel less alone in the endeavour of leading well. These influences from our own lives form a part of our story that will have influenced our outlooks, values, and opinions to varying degrees, and which are important elements that will have mostly subconsciously, but sometimes even consciously, shaped how we show up, respond, think – and indeed lead. Each of those we work with have stories and journeys relevant and influential to the way they present, too. Some of those are more useful than we might first imagine. While the notion that we all have a story to tell is universally agreeable, not enough leaders know their team's current story let alone the chapters that went before.

What skills, talents or experiences do they possess that you or the wider organisation aren't utilising?

When running culture programs or my 'Leadership Actions and Behaviours' workshop, we explore what skills and attributes would be useful to achieve the organisation's aims, or to resolve current challenges. Commonly identified responses are problem solving, better communication, stronger collaboration, and clarity in strategic direction. Then we look for where those skills might exist that haven't been explored before, such as in other teams or in maintenance or hospitality teams. "Who else can we learn from?" is a question that keeps us levelling up, and one I've helped to integrate into high performing sports teams. I encourage it to be asked, and answered, monthly, providing twelve opportunities each year to continue to enhance performance in new and complimentary areas.

My job demands that I travel a lot. On a flight to Greece, I spent a delightful few hours talking with a former senior military

General from Turkey who spoke very little English. Fortunately, his wife was able to translate, for which I was especially thankful, allowing me to hear his remarkable story. Since arriving in England as a refugee escaping exile, he had worked several low paid, menial jobs as a warehouse picker, a pot washer, and a kitchen assistant. He told me how he had been turned down by many employers because of his inability to speak good English but that regardless no one had asked him what he was capable of, or what experience he had. He was reduced to accepting jobs which language wasn't a barrier for, for him to be able to provide for his family. His harrowing story of attempting to escape a military coup, being caught, and captured, imprisoned, threatened, and given twenty-four hours to disappear isn't mine to tell. It would make for a gripping Hollywood blockbuster, though. On his second attempt, he was successful, hiding under the seat of a car as he and a friend crossed the border, and then proceeding on foot through three countries, eventually making his way to England. I asked his wife to translate for me a question I ask anyone I meet who has held a senior leadership position: "What did he think was the most important lesson he has learnt about good leadership?". The former General looked off into the distance and considered my question. His eyes became glassy as he responded in Turkish: "We do not know what tomorrow brings, so use every day to strengthen our team and encourage them to do their very best. When you are no longer their leader, you will be able to look back fondly on your legacy of helping people to be and do their best". Since meeting the former General, who I'm intentionally withholding the name of, I have begun to encourage leaders to consider where the attributes they have identified as being especially useful to them may already exist within their team. For example, the cleaning or catering team are unlikely to have been invited to a strategy day, and yet they may well possess useful skills, experiences, and talents outside of their employed role that could make a difference. If any of those individuals have experience as a volunteer police officer, or retained firefighter, for example, they will have problem solving, conflict resolution skills, and communication training that could be of great value and use to you. What if their story put them in the employed position you know them for, and not their capability? I talk a lot to people I meet, at almost every opportunity and in an unusually quiet airport lounge I met Akita who kindly took my empty plate and cleaned my table. After polite conversation, I asked her what her story was, and she explained she was in England to help improve her English for future career prospects. "What would you like to do?", I asked Akita. I'm not sure what I expected her answer to be, but I'm certain it wasn't this: "I have a degree in hospitality and a PhD in social psychology but I'm unsure what I want to do – possibly something different again but I do want my English to be better." I asked her if the management of the airport or lounge had ever invited her to meetings, or to be involved with strategy or training? Dr. Akita wiped the table, looked at me confused and paused. "No?". She was employed to clear tables and wipe them. That was the context of her employment, so that's what she showed up to do.

On July 1st, 2010, Thomas William Simpson died in Norfolk aged eighty. Born in London, he became revered as one of the most important minds in the field of magic and specifically the subspecialty known as mentalism, writing what is still considered one of the great magic books of all time and a must-read for any serious mental magic artist. At Thomas's funeral, a man stood mourning his friend, puzzled by having met so many magicians among the mourners. Almost everyone he spoke with was a magician. It transpired Thomas was also a champion chess player, the friend his chess partner. Not once, however, had Thomas mentioned his life as a magician, inventor, and author of magic effects, nor had he performed for his friend. It is remarkable that Thomas lived so humbly, with no one in the magic community knowing of his remarkable chess skills, nor any of his chess companions knowing just how important he was to magicians the world over. The next time you look out at those in your charge, consider the things you don't know about them. What have they not offered because you haven't asked? We tend to only answers the questions we are asked.

In *Flip the Switch* I wrote about how the globally loved Kellogg's Variety Pack product came about; those eight, small, individual boxes of cereal so loved by holidaying parents. It was the brainchild of one Harold Muntz, not as part of his job as a new product engineer, or a role in marketing, but in response to a newly implemented company-wide suggestions box. In 1938 "he felt that many people already familiar with individual size packages through sampling, and the use of 'individuals' in restaurants, would jump at the opportunity to buy a variety of these small packages for home use". The rest is history. Often when I stand before an audience and look out at the faces staring back at me, a brief chill runs over me. Someone in that room may well have a thought, experience, or knowledge that could revolutionise the organisation or change their fortunes in much the same way Muntz did for Kellogg's. Uncover what more you have to offer by asking those in your charge for their ideas and input regularly but build on that to create something better still by asking: "What else?". I'll discuss elsewhere what this does to our teams, and how we shouldn't fear appearing less of a leader, or without command, or indeed lacking our own ideas, which is a common concern often cited. Suffice to say it does quite the opposite, strengthening both teams and our cultures.

Many things make us change: coercion, desire, circumstance, environment, force, desperation, and time, for example. We are changing all the time. Ten-year-old you, was not the same as twenty-year-old you. When you reach thirty, you've changed again and are different to when you were twenty. Ten years on at forty, your values, outlooks, boundaries, tastes etc are different again. We don't only change in ten-year cycles, but sometimes daily, and occasionally multiple times in a day. An especially stirring documentary on food, for example, that shines a light onto your current eating preferences may well prompt you to change out of disgust, desire, or enlightenment. Once presented with the facts and having watched documentaries that supported my concerns for the welfare of animals, and the subsequent hygiene issues in the food chain in America, I opted to become vegetarian - overnight. We can and do change frequently yet we still resist the notion of change, almost exclusively because of a combination of fear of the unknown, and a lack of information presented to support the reasoning for change. Post-Covid many organisations are encouraging, and some insisting, a return to the workplace, putting an end to the work from home culture. According to Business Transition 360, sixty eight percent of employers believe workers should return for at least three days a week and yet only three percent of employees wish to return to the office for a full week. Most employees want a hybrid working model. Why? We adapt and evolve readily to change. Cast your mind back to the pandemic and working from home was what almost everyone was struggling with. Never mind trying to maintain a metre apart from people, millions of people worldwide were struggling enough to maintain their attention, motivation, communication, efficiency, and concentration whilst doing their job. With the associated serious health risk and global comradery to pull together and fight the infection, there was little resistance to the changes imposed upon us and subsequently we readily adapted. So much so that most are now quite happy with this new way of working that few would have ever believed would have ever worked prior to 1999. When we have the information we need to understand the changes required, we can and do adapt. We do so because our species is fantastic at it.

Change is of course an inevitable force in the landscape of leadership. There's no escaping it, whether we lead a small team, a non-profit organization, or a multinational corporation, our ability to navigate and embrace change will define our effectiveness as a leader. In a world characterized by rapid technological advancements, shifting market dynamics, and evolving societal expectations, understanding the importance of change isn't just beneficial; it's essential.

My personal preference when working in the change space is to keep in mind that, at its core, change is a process that alters the status quo, and that it can be incremental or transformative, planned, or spontaneous. It keeps it technical and literal when change can often be highly emotionally charged. Separating emotion from fact, in this case, can be especially useful. The key to successfully managing change lies in recognizing its dual nature: it is both a challenge and an opportunity. Leaders who see change as an opportunity are more likely to inspire their teams to innovate and adapt, fostering a culture that thrives on flexibility and resilience. Those who don't foster teams who are fearful, anxious, and much more likely to resist, making everything to do with working with them much more difficult and complicated.

One of the greatest challenges to face leaders is the psychological barrier that change often presents. Humans are creatures of habit, finding comfort in routine. When that routine is disrupted, anxiety often arises. I know from personal experience just how much of a creature of habit I am, and how much comfort, reassurance and indeed calm, it offers me. For many years I resisted change but wasn't aware of it. It took a life crisis to force reflection and a personal discovery journey to become more conscious of my behaviours. It was an enlightening experience that enhanced my ability to work more effectively with change, having experienced it from 'the other side'. Acknowledging fears is crucial. However, it can be challenging for leaders who do not necessarily share or see those fears. When we cultivate an environment where team members feel safe to express their concerns about change, we foster open dialogue and understanding and the hard work of knowing what others are thinking or feeling is done for us.

I think most people would agree that effective communication is a cornerstone of leadership, but especially so during periods of change. Clarity is vital when conveying changes, in as much detail is possible and appropriate; leaders should articulate the reasons behind them and the expected outcomes. It is this transparency which alleviates anxiety and empowers teams: when we understand the "why" behind a change, we are more likely to buy into the process and engage positively. Often I see a 'catch-all' approach to communication, probably because it's easier, which really only reveals laziness and a lack of humanity. Utilizing various communication channels is also essential, as different team members may respond better to different modes of communication, be it meetings, emails, or informal discussion. Tailoring messages to the audience enhances their reception and effectiveness.

The majority of clients who approach me to work with them through a change, whatever the specifics are, present a change that will take time. Rarely are the changes straightforward or quick fixes. To lead effectively through change, cultivating a change-ready culture is paramount. This begins with modeling adaptability ourselves. Demonstrating flexibility in our leadership style and decision-making processes encourages our teams to experiment, take risks, and learn from failures. It is the cornerstone of the human-centred leadership approach. Celebrate not just successes but also the lessons learned from setbacks: in turn change is viewed as a necessary – and, importantly, normal - component of growth.

As you may well have experienced or witnessed, during times of change, emotions can run high, and a leader's ability to empathize can be the difference between helping to diffuse tension and build trust, or creating deeper resentment, hatred, and resistance. During my research I have read and dipped into many old books on leadership and the notion that "it's lonely at the top" is one I am beginning to understand now is simply because they made it so by the way they led.

Let's be honest, change can be incredible. More often than not, even changes that are uncomfortable or initially unwelcome, often lead to better things; they a fundamental part of our life journeys. It's resisted so often because of the threat to our identity and safety that change has the potential to cause but more often than not acts as a catalyst for innovation. Organizations that embrace change are more likely to develop new ideas, products, and services and so it could be argued that it is our responsibility as leaders to encourage a culture of innovation by creating an environment where experimentation is valued. Experimentation, of course, is a different word for change: by virtue of the act of experimenting we are trying something new; doing something different. If we can set aside time for creative thinking, promoting cross-functional collaboration, and providing incentives for innovative ideas, we in turn foster a mindset of continuous improvement. It is this subtle behavioural shift that drives innovation; encourages your team to evaluate processes regularly and seek ways to enhance efficiency and effectiveness. By positioning change as a pathway to innovation rather than a disruption, we help our teams see the potential benefits of adapting to new circumstances. Ultimately coming to be inquisitive of, welcome and embrace change.

Celebrating change is essential to fostering a positive outlook on the process. Acknowledge milestones achieved during transitions, no matter how small – don't wait to save them for annual recognition events. Recognition can come in various forms and should be personalised to be relevant and reinforcing to the individual, such as team celebrations, shout-outs in meetings, or personal rewards for those who contribute significantly to the change process. By celebrating change, we reinforce the idea that adapting, and evolving is a collective effort. You'll struggle to find many more efficacious ways to boost morale and strengthen team cohesion.

Change is not merely a challenge to be managed; it is an integral part of the leadership journey. As a leader, our ability to navigate and embrace change can transform not only our organizations but also the lives of those we lead. That is a considered remark. By cultivating a change-ready culture, communicating effectively, and fostering innovation, we can inspire our teams to view change as an opportunity for growth, development, and potential, rather than a disruption, or anxiety-ridden threat.

In a world that is constantly evolving, the leaders who thrive will be those who are willing to embrace change, adapt, and inspire their teams to do the same, even when it isn't their idea.

When we want to change, we're quite happy to dye our hair, shave it off, change careers, or get a pet after a lifetime of saying we never would. When the change isn't our idea or comes at a time or point in our life when we may not be ready, we meet resistance - and when we don't have enough information to readily embrace or understand the reason for changing, it triggers an instinctive reaction to help keep us safe, which is to stay put. We know where we are works for us (if it does), and so if we're given the choice, we're more likely to resist the notion of change. What many organisations are doing is ignorant of this and simply changing the rules; overnight demanding that people change their now long-established patterns and routines for them. As one union representative put it when asked how people felt about being forced to return to work: "They are outraged". We can be gentle and ease people into a new schedule, but the real issue is the lack of information: the why. At the centre of all behaviour change – and indeed my career – is the simple question: Why do we do the things we do, and how can we change them for the better? When we can offer suitable explanation, it helps will people to want to change.

Remember, change is not the enemy; it is the catalyst for progress. Without sufficient explanation that is acceptable and understood, we unintentionally create conflict.

5
The Absence of Conflict.

"The greatest discovery of all time is that a person can change his future by merely changing his attitude."

Oprah Winfrey

'Conflict management' is a popular phrase in corporate parlance that makes me uncomfortable. It's the management word again. The idea of coping with conflict doesn't inspire a huge amount of confidence. Having said that, I'm not keen on the conflict part either; it creates a negative connotation from the outset. Conflict resolution is marginally better, but that emotionally charged 'conflict' still stands out. In a world where conflict is happening all the time to varying degrees and results, from a misinterpreted email tone to all-out war, putting emphasis on something that is an expected outcome of occasional human interaction by virtue of humans living and working in proximity, dramatizes it unnecessarily. Conflict management is really nothing more than effective communication skills. With strong cultures, clear values, and improved communication ability, much conflict we see in the workplace can be self-resolved, or at the very least self-managed. Applying a grandiose name only serves to make it more of an issue than it really is but as with many corporate buzzwords, few questions are asked to challenge the usefulness of their presence, let alone explore their true meaning. Humans will not always see eye to eye, or indeed play nicely, and it falls to leaders to help manage those situations.

The success of managing conflict relies on an understanding of the field of emotional intelligence and the role it plays in being able to effectively diffuse the tension, and resolution of, challenging situations. I would argue the diffusion is the most important part of this resolution triad. Too many of us are quick to react and respond without consideration of the circumstances and consequences of our response, and certainly without effort in managing the situation and the response of others involved. Hunger, tiredness, stress, and pain are just a few causes I'm sure most can relate to which can influence a quickness and ill-measured response leading to heightened tension and conflict. I'm very much a morning person, waking around five each morning, but not overly approachable before I've had my coffee and some food, and certainly less tolerant on anything less than eight hours sleep. I can feel the difference in myself and am conscious of how much harder I need to try when hungry or tired – and I dread being both, as do my team! We see this at home with our partners when they innocently ask if we can tidy something away, only to find ourselves delivering a cutting, passive-aggressive response: the tiredness or stress driving our response, and certainly not a considered response. The resolution is simple at home and at work, as resolutions to many of our behaviour challenges are, and it was Mickey Mouse who showed me the impact this simple technique has. When I worked with the Walt Disney Company, I was struck with how almost impossible it was to be angry with Mickey Mouse. The perpetually smiley, energetic, waving mouse, happy to be dressed in bright red shorts responds with his cute little shoulder shrug, or an exaggerated wave, and a great big, permanent wide-eyed smile. You might initially be irritated by him, but I'd struggle to understand how anyone could become angry with the personification of anger diffusion. Mickey, if I may be so informal, is a role model worth recalling before we react. It's a four-step process that is as simple as it is effective, and one you'll likely be familiar with because many of the most effective ways to manage behaviour are both simple and familiar:

Stop. Listen. Reflect. Respond.

If it is that simple to help avert conflict, why are we so regularly finding ourselves engaged in it?

Research conducted by Lubit in 2004 showed the more emotionally intelligent someone is, the more likely they are to resolve conflict. Therefore, working on enhancing our awareness of emotional intelligence will naturally benefit our ability to deal with conflict and has many wider benefits for those we live and work with, and for our own personal happiness, too.

The three questions all leaders should have in the toolkit to aid rapid resolution of conflict are:

1. *What is the source of the conflict?*

2. *What is it that has created the emotional response leading to their conflict?*

3. *What does this mean to them?*

Conflict is most often a result of frustration. A feeling that stems from a lack of control, a lack of knowledge, understanding, and compassion. When broken down in this way we can better see it for what it is: behaviours don't simply happen; they are caused. Look for, or at least consider, the trigger, the source - the antecedent. We spend a lot of wasted time dealing with behaviours themselves without an understanding of their cause but when we seek to understand causes it is easier to rectify and prevent the conflict from arising again. That is not to say that dealing with undesirable behaviour is a waste of time, but that we spend more time than is necessary worrying over, managing, contemplating, and being consumed or distracted by the behaviour more than its cause. Behaviours will continue to appear if the cause, or causes, are still present.

High performing individuals and teams I work with are taught to start at the end, considering the desired consequences and outcomes, then to uncover which behaviours will help support that goal, and finally to calculate how to influence those behaviours to happen. This is a standard behaviour model, which we will explore more fully in another chapter. Working our way through the sequence of behaviours in this way is beneficial also for effective leadership. Considering a behaviour model such as this helps prevent us from becoming distracted by the behaviours themselves, and a framework like this helps prevent us focusing on the wrong thing. Consider how a child continuously tugs at our clothing to get our attention. Barking at them for tugging, or poking, or otherwise being annoying is often the first response to their behaviour. However, when our attention is raised by their tugging, the first consideration should by why this behaviour is happening: What do they need our attention for? Are they urgently in need of the toilet? Are they thirsty, or injured? Once established, we can then model the desired behaviour: *"You're bored? Ok, well, in the future if you need my attention please don't tug at my clothes; say excuse me Daddy to get my attention, okay?".* If the tugging at our clothing was to bring attention to the escaped lion, or truck hurtling towards the window, or broken lamp they'd just knocked over, the behaviour, however, irritating in isolation, would have been a welcome alert to our immediate attention. Behaviours are modelled, or shaped, by their consequences but without effective modelling we simply get more of whatever behaviours we reinforce or feed – intentionally or not. In this example, giving in to the child is attention, all-be-it not especially kind if we snap at them, and if we continue to reinforce the behaviour by giving them our attention, the annoying behaviours of tugging at clothes or poking will continue. Often, we're unaware of it consciously, but we are all modelling behaviours in ourselves and others by how we respond and which behaviours we encourage or discourage by giving them our attention, or not.

Models that help keep us focused are an integral and key element to the field of medicine. In chaotic and confusing situations where emotions regularly run high, it is essential for leaders to remain calm and focused when making decisions. Many of the models used in modern medicine have been adopted from military models and one person was key in devising and popularising many of them, and subsequently responsible for saving countless lives throughout his career: Professor Timothy Hodgetts CB, CBE, KHS, DL. At the time of writing, he is the United Kingdom's Surgeon General; Master General of the Army Medical Services for the British Army; Chair for the Committee of Military Medical Chiefs in NATO; Deputy Lieutenant for the County of West Midlands and Visiting Professor of the Military Medical Academy in Belgrade. He is also a Consultant in Emergency Medicine. How he found the time to talk with me I will never know!

I first met Tim about ten years ago at a company conference we had both been invited to speak at. Having a background in medicine, I immediately recognised Tim's name as a highly respected exemplar of phenomenal leadership and clinical ability. I had admired his thinking, creativity, and career for many years, and since leaving medicine had not heard of his name again, so I was especially excited to hear him speak about applying his clinical leadership experiences in warzones, to corporate leadership. It complimented my own presentation on the behavioural science of effective leadership. Several years later at a different conference I introduced Tim in my capacity as host. He was one of the first people I reached out to when writing this book, with a real hope he'd agree to be interviewed because he has a calm, measured, and well-considered approach to leadership. His analytical and problem-solving mindset nurtured through his practice of medicine has been applied to his role as a leader, which he takes equally as seriously as his role of clinician. This is evident by his impressive promotions to seriously senior appointments, but also in his writing on the importance of leadership as a professional role, with a need for professional development and serious study for it to be truly effective.

I asked Tim if there were any leaders from his own life that had perhaps had an impact on him, and on the way he leads. *"Professor Harold Ellis was one of the professors from my medical school and was genuinely inspiring to me. He was such a powerful teacher, and I loved his teaching style, but he also wrote some of the best books for students – and they were the best because they were so simple to understand. So logical, simple to digest, and therefore memorable. When you're trying to get your head around real complex issues you need a simple framework to analyse every patient and remember the key causes of particular symptom sets, for example. I've taken a lot from that and throughout my career been a serial simplifier. In hindsight it probably came from quite a selfish place, from wanting to make things as simple as possible to help me to do better; to help patients more easily. So, while these simplifications were initially for me, I realised they were very helpful for others, too, and it's thanks to Harold Ellis really that this focus on simplifying unnecessarily complex issues came about."* Tim's being a little modest here as he's probably single-handedly responsible for more medical acronyms, which act as aide-memoires to ensure the correct information is transmitted effectively, than any other person, and has been a key figure in the wide adoption of emergency medical training.

As Tim spoke of the leaders who had made a positive impact on him, and his own leadership style, a similarity struck me: they were each passing on information to the next generation, whether implicitly or explicitly. There was a motivation to pass on information. This has been a recurring theme in each of the interviews I conducted with senior leaders for research while writing this book but also echoes my own experiences both in my personal career of leaders I have experienced who have positively influenced me, and professionally now in my capacity advising, training, and coaching leaders. The most effective are those who understand that leadership is not about them; a characteristic almost never seen in the more common arrogant, narcissistic, and lazy qualities leadership is commonly strangled by. Truly effective and memorable leaders understand their role is to help lift others up: to advance together through the enablement of those around them.

Tim's own concerns surrounding the importance of certain characteristics for effective leaders echo my own. He believes the most important characteristics, especially in crisis management where Tim's own career has seen him spend so much time, are:

Decisiveness
Determination
Vision
Curiosity, and
Preparation.

His opinions on this are supported by first-hand experience. While serving in Hannover at a military hospital - where Tim was also exposed to his first experience of terrorism - bombs and attacks were a frequent occurrence by the active Irish Republican Army (IRA), which Tim and his medical colleagues saw the tragic results of. One day in particular a coded bomb warning was telephoned through to the hospital. Imagine for a moment you are in Tim's position as the department leader. You've no reason to believe this wasn't going to be like any other normal day. You are carrying on with your usual workload when the telephone rings; your colleague answers it, and you're informed what the anonymous voice has said. Given the activity surrounding the hospital locality, you acknowledge that it's a credible bomb threat.

You must decide based on the information you have: do you evacuate the building? Or do you remain and not evacuate?

What would you do?

Perhaps you don't know; that's a third option both here in this recollection of the scenario, but also at the time.

Tim's response was stark: *"The correct answer is evacuate. Or don't evacuate. The incorrect answer is 'I don't know'.*

You must decide with bounded rationality. As Colin Powell explains in his forty-seventy principle, if you haven't got forty percent of the information, you probably can't make a safe decision, but if you've waited until you've got more than seventy percent then the enemy may have already acted. And in medicine, the enemy is often time: if you don't act quickly enough the patient will have deteriorated. You must decide and begin to treat, and as new information comes in you must be emergent and make new decisions to possibly change the direction. Nicholas Colnet, physician to Henry V, said: "The mark of a mature mind is to bear uncertainty with equanimity". With high certainty and high agreement, you probably don't need leaders because things will just happen. It's when there is high uncertainty and high disagreement that leadership really comes into its own and has the most effect." Tim explains how in his role as Chair for the NATO Committee of Military Medical Chiefs, he has seen this play out first hand: *"New motions or changes can only be passed with unanimous consensus, so very often things take time, and everyone must work together to ensure we all have all of the information we each require to make a decision. When we don't have the luxury of time, our leadership skills must be efficient and effective to achieve a unanimous decision quickly."*

Being able to adapt and embrace change is a skill leaders must be comfortable with, but it isn't one that comes naturally to us. The human being is inherently resistant to change, and it's almost impossible to work in the fields of psychology or behaviour without having to consider and manage our relationship with it. It's become an area of fascination, and subsequent specialty of mine and a core focus of my work. Tim's own advice comes from professional setbacks in his career where he knew he had improvements that would help save lives but was met with resistance to change. One determined campaign saw Tim push for twenty years before his ideas were met with acceptance and understanding, and subsequent widespread global application. *"If you morally believe it's the right thing to do, keep going. Vision can be a curse; you can know this is the right thing to do but to try to pull people along who cannot see in that same way and who see things in a more linear and incremental way can be frustrating, especially if you need to move fast."* Much of Tim's leadership learning has been done during, and influenced by, times of crisis management and traumatic events: ballistic incidents; war; treating trauma patients; bombings; serious accidents – it's a niche workplace. However, the common thread is people. The learnings can be directly applied to a school, or office, or factory, for example. Those environments will be significantly less acutely stressful and traumatic (one would hope!), yet the people problems and challenges will remain similar or the same.

Our aim as leaders should be to resolve conflict. Often when I am working with a senior leadership team or organisation in an advisory role to assist with conflict, their attention is on the specific things said, or done, and the behaviours taking full spotlight. To focus there is only a small part of the issue: our primary aim is to address the antecedent. Where has this conflict come from, and how to do we minimise it, then look to resolve it? If you did nothing else, in turn you are likely to get what is known as 'behaviour extinction'. Without a reinforcer for a behaviour, something that encourages and feeds it – such as a hostile situation or ongoing conflict – we see more of that behaviour. Remove that reinforcer and the behaviour extinguishes on its own. When looking to resolve conflict, first determine an answer to what resolution looks like for them. Be clear about the desired consequence. Once everyone has had their say, and feels heard, we can work towards finding an agreeable middle ground, reinforcing that, and modelling behaviours to support a positive change that subsequently also reinforces the resolution. This is the mark of emotionally intelligent leaders.

It is widely accepted that there are five characteristics of emotionally intelligent people:

Empathy
Social skills
Self-awareness
Self-regulation, and
Motivation.

Which do you think is the most important?

They are all important, but it is my opinion that self-awareness is the most important. Without self-awareness we are unable to self-regulate. We cannot effectively monitor motivation of self, or others; we wouldn't know if we were being empathetic, or how good we were at it, and would certainly be unable to assess or improve our social skills. Yet, many leaders I meet are on auto pilot. They have the title, the status, the responsibility, the pay increase, and the workload. While they may be interested in reading around the subject of self-help and leadership, they have in effect finished trying. If leadership, and especially senior leadership, is the goal then where else is there to go when you've achieved that?

Marshall Goldsmith' second example of a leader that especially influenced him was Frances Hesselbein; possibly one of the most underrated leaders of all time. She most famously served as CEO of Girl Scouts of America. She was awarded twenty -two honorary doctoral degrees, co-edited thirty-five books, wrote several of her own, and established an internationally respected leadership movement.

Frances had asked Marshall to give some talks to some of the Girl Scout staff. When the time came to deliver the agreed talks, he found himself extremely busy with speaking engagements, hotel hopping from one engagement to the next. He enquired with Frances if there was anywhere nearby where he might get his clothes cleaned. Frances reassured him there were on-site laundry facilities – all he needed to do was leave his dirty laundry on the floor, and someone would take them to the laundry and have them cleaned. The morning after having this conversation with Frances, Marshall was stood in a corridor talking to the regional heads of Girl Scouts of America when Frances walked past carrying Marshall's pile of dirty clothes to the laundry room. *"Every person saw her. She didn't say a thing. She didn't have to give a speech about subservient leadership – she was the speech. The last time I saw her before she died, she was 107. I assumed I'd be saying goodbye to a very elderly woman in a coma, or at best asleep. She knew she was dying; could barely eat and had difficulty breathing. In fact, she sat and smiled and talked with me for twenty minutes about one thing: me. The entire conversation was aimed at me. The thing about Frances, and Alan, I never, after hundreds of hours in their company, heard either of them complain about anything. If you're in a leadership role, it's show time. There's no time for "poor me"; "my headache hurts", or for it to be about you, and that's not being a phony; in my book that's being a professional. Leadership isn't about focusing on what you need; it's about focusing on what they need."*

I asked Marshall what he believed were the most important characteristics for effective leaders. As one might expect from someone voted the World's Number 1 Leadership Thinker, his response was detailed, however, centred around five main points:

Global thinking
A positive attitude toward cultural diversity
Technological savviness
Building alliances and partnerships, and
Thinking like a facilitator not a director.

Focusing on these is key, especially for leaders of the near future to fully engage younger generations for who have grown up in a technologically advanced, exceptionally connected, diversely cultural landscape built on collaboration and partnerships. Easier for new generations of leaders to understand, but what of existing leaders, especially those working with young generations in their teams? One of Marshall's remedies for this, is to ask regular questions of ourselves that help us focus on being and doing better, in turn putting the ownership of personal and professional development on us. *"As Arnold Schwarzenegger said: "I don't build muscle by looking at the weights". You must lift the weights, and lifting the weights is hard.*

Working on leadership is hard, but you can't just read the books, you must do the work. Here are six questions we can ask that help us to remain focused:

1. *Set clear goals: "Have I set clear, actionable goals to achieve the outcome or behaviours I need to see?"*

2. *Make progress through achieving my goals: "How well did I do today? How much closer am I to my goal?"*

3. *Be happy: "How happy am I?"*

4. *Find meaning: "Did today have some semblance of meaning for me? Where do I find meaning?"*

5. *Build positive relationships: "Who can help me, and how can I help them?"*

6. *Be fully engaged: "How engaged was I today on a scale of 1-10?"""*

Marshall cautions the inevitable that comes with a position of leadership, even when the individual may be selfless and inclusive: what leaders say very often become orders. Whether it's good or bad, or right, or wrong, it will become an order by virtue that it was said by you. The responsibility is greater than you may imagine, and the astute leaders understand this. It's principally easy to understand but challenging to do. It is so effective to bring your team on board, asking for their thoughts, ideas, opinions, and to regularly ask questions. The lesson is to stop before you respond. Breathe. Pause. Consider that whatever you say will become an order, and ask yourself if perhaps, as Alan Mulally taught Marshall, the response might be best delivered as a question.

The right questions are the cornerstone of effective leadership. Knowing which to ask and when, is the difference between ordinary and high performance.

6
A Brief Scientific Encounter.

"What you do makes a difference. You have to decide what kind of a difference you want to make."

Jane Goodall

The behaviour model (antecedent > behaviour > consequence) is a simple chain that helps us to understand and model all mammalian behaviour. Societal influences have encouraged us to become much more reactive and in turn less proactive in almost every way: same-day delivery, no-quibble returns, and one-click checkout processes are common examples of how our expectations, demands, and focuses are manipulated long-term, impacting how we respond in life elsewhere. We get more of the behaviours we feed, so feeding impatience and high expectations of immediate results only causes frustration and anger when they are not realised. We are unknowingly being taught to be less tolerant, less patient, less understanding, and less compassionate when we interact with many of the most unlikely of spaces. It remains much more efficacious to focus first on the desired consequence, then to consider the behaviours that will help us achieve that, and finally to consider how we influence the right behaviours. That considered approach takes a fractional amount more effort and time, which is at odds with what many of us are now used to. Subsequently, we see more people jump straight to attempting to manage a behaviour, dealing with the consequences later.

This same impatience manifests in shaping behaviours through their consequences, in the form of punishment and reinforcement. I am a proponent for patient reinforcement; a strategy with benefits for us as well as those we are helping to model. However, it is undeniably most often much easier and quicker to punish – and we do. A lot. We shout, snap, bark, fire off passive or directly aggressive emails and texts, punch, hit, shoot, stab, and throw. I'm using the collective "we" to mean our species; personally, I'm a pacifist. Consider walking along the hallway of your home. As you pass a room you casually look in and see your child sat calmly reading a book, or your dog peacefully laid on the floor. Very few of us would take the opportunity to praise and reinforce the clearly desirable calm behaviour: "Good girl for sitting there calmly and reading a book while Daddy gets on with some housework". "Good dog – good settle". We often take for granted desirable behaviours when they are presented. Yet, consider this alternative situation: As you walk past the room and look in, your darling little girl is redecorating with a discovered lipstick, or rubbing chocolate into the carpet. Perhaps the dog is humping the couch and tearing apart a cushion. We would surely find the time to deliver a punishment and raise our voice to show our disapproval. In so many ways it is sad to see what we have become. As Maude laments in *Harold and Maude*: "zoos are full, prisons are overflowing. My, my. How the world still dearly loves a cage." How disconnected we are from being present, subconsciously manipulated by the ability to post or check social media for fear of missing out or being validated or check news outlets encouraged by unchecked habits. Our habits are largely shaped by our environment. Content is created and changing at a pace quicker than we can keep up. According to Forbes, in two years alone, between 2016 and 2018, ninety percent of the data in the world at the time was generated. Leadership now is in many ways unrecognisable than it was only ten years ago. I don't mean in terms of dress sense, salary, technology, and expectations – although those have all changed, too. The way people behave, respond, and the people challenges leaders must have the tools to effectively manage today is wildly different. Society is different because of the society we are creating. My writing this book is contributing to the very problem I'm writing about. We are obsessively creating data, which is vicariously indirectly modelling our behaviour because of what we do with that data. What we need is leaders who better understand human behaviour, to help support and shape their people. We need to talk more about how we equip leaders with efficacious people skills and that begins by talking more about punishment and reinforcement – especially in the context of the workplace.

Leaders must better understand both and efficacious ways of using them. If we get more behaviours by feeding them, or reinforcing them, conversely, we get less of the behaviours we punish.

The notion of punishment in the workplace is generally shied away from. When I mention it in meetings you can often feel the atmosphere immediately tense. I suspect it is because the word has especially negative connotations. We often think of punitive measures when we consider punishment: hitting, isolation, torture even. Being the cat among the pigeons can be fun, and I imagine clients visualising people in the office running towards an individual brandishing forks from the canteen, duct tape and desk staplers screaming: "punish him!". However, punishment, just like reinforcement, can be achieved by adding something to the situation, or removing it. Let's start with the technical definitions.

Reinforcement is an act that increases the frequency of the immediately preceding behaviour.

Punishment is an act that reduces or eliminates the immediately preceding behaviour.

That's it. As complicated as we like us to be, we are fundamentally quite simple.

There is, however, one caveat.

Both punishments and reinforcements are subjective. What one person finds punitive; another may well find reinforcing. Indeed, yet another may be entirely ambivalent to either punisher or reinforcer. At a global conference some years ago, I witnessed the uncomfortable definition of this. Just before I was invited to the stage to deliver my speech, several key internal awards were presented to demonstrate recognition. One of which was the highly coveted 'Customer Service Agent of the Year' award. A humongous basket of chocolate about the size and weight of a small child was caried out by two people, so heavy and cumbersome was the prize. It was presented proudly and with much applause, to a lady I'll never forget meeting late, named Dawn. It is fair to say Dawn looked more than a little perturbed.

In fact, I'd describe her expression and attitude as mightily cheesed off. She walked to the stage with the demeanour of someone who had just been issued divorce proceedings, shook the hand of the award host, and returned to her seat followed by her two colleagues carrying the gigantic basket of chocolate. As soon as I finished speaking, I made a bee line for Dawn. I wanted to know what the reasons for her clear discontent were at having been presented with what to some would be a lifetime's supply of delicious chocolate. Dawn, as it turns out, had not only worked at the company for fifteen years, but was diabetic. And everyone at the company knew. At that moment in time Dawn felt the most undervalued, underappreciated, and unseen she had ever felt. The award was intended as a reinforcement; that's why companies give rewards: to recognise behaviours they would like to see more of. In this case, they may well have unintentionally punished Dawn, for they certainly did not reinforce her.

In 2009 my team and I conducted a very simple research project via an online questionnaire. We sent it to my newsletter list consisting of delegates from conferences in the various countries I'd presented in, asking which actions they would feel most reinforced by and therefore more likely to repeat a behaviour. The questions specifically looked at effort: what would encourage you to continue to put in maximum effort? The options offered were all genuine things I knew my current list of clients were using cash, gift cards, a bottle of Champagne, paid dinner for two, and a half day off. We added another somewhat less materialistic option: a hand-written letter of appreciation and thanks from the company CEO. Way ahead as the reinforcer our small sample of three thousand respondents said would encourage them most to continue to put in more effort, was the letter from the CEO. The take home message for all leaders is to ask what those in their charge find most rewarding. Discover what their reinforces are. For some it will be validation in the form of verbal praise. Others want your time, and others still want material value.

If reinforcement and punishment are individually subjective, they are also time sensitive. One of the reasons our prisons are consistently overflowing and why reoffending rates remain so high is because the punishment itself doesn't happen at the correct time. If I suddenly snapped and went off the rails, going on a mugging spree, tripping up elderly women and running off with their handbags, I'd hopefully be arrested and detained. I say hopefully in the sense of having faith in the law enforcement system, not that I have a particularly niche fetish. So far so good in terms of our behaviour chain: the behaviour has a consequence. If it was my first crime and I was new to the world of grab and run, the encounter with law enforcement might well be sufficient punishment and effectively deter me from repeating the behaviour. However, for many individuals and their crimes it clearly isn't deterrent enough. We have prisons with unsafe numbers of inmates, insufficient staff to manage the burgeoning numbers, and little room for more - and this is where the efficacy of a consequence starts to come undone. From the moment of me acting out my illegal behaviour to the point of actual punishment in the form of a prison sentence, for example, isolated from friends and family and with many social privileges removed, it can be many months, in some cases years. Remember the definition of a punishment: an act that reduces or eliminates the *immediately preceding* behaviour. To be effective, consequences for our actions need to happen as soon as possible following the behaviour. The very first time I touched a hot iron, I immediately received feedback and a consequence in the form of a physically unpleasant burning sensation. It discouraged me from willingly doing that again and makes me more cautious and careful when using an iron now. However, if my iron punishment was delivered in the same schedule as my mugging, I'd touch an iron on Monday morning and suddenly receive a burning sensation several months later, making it unlikely or impossible to link the original behaviour to the correlating consequence. Indeed, it is likely to be linked to whatever I happened to be doing immediately before the burning sensation was felt, deterring me from doing that again, no matter how irrelevant. It is for this reason I believe annual awards and recognition events are particularly ineffective – indeed any form of feedback that is saved up for an annual outing: the longer the gap between behaviour and consequence, the less efficacious the consequence. In much the same way, many relationships at home are ineffective or strained. With our children and partners, we don't communicate enough, nor well enough. Withholding information or feedback, opting instead for passive aggressive remarks, or to see if they will notice something, for example, as if part of a test, doesn't help with the feedback loop that effective communication so critically relies on.

The role of a leader is to lead people. Yet many have poor understanding of how people work. It doesn't make sense. Why haven't we been teaching leaders why we do the things we do and how to change them for the better? Why haven't we given our leaders the knowledge and tools required to better understand and guide the humans in their charge? We have been far too distracted by pointless personality profiling, and leadership systems and processes for far too long now. We need to begin *thinking* like psychologists and *behaving* like leaders.

The American psychologist Carl Rogers coined the phrase "person-centred psychotherapy". Rogers' specific approach was based on his belief that people are inherently driven toward, and have the capacity for, growth and self-actualisation. It focuses on the process and that to be truly person-centred is process driven. One must trust the processes that are congruent and that the outcomes will take care of themselves. In my experience, it is rare that leaders have the confidence or support to trust the process and therefore be truly person-centred. They are more commonly focused on outcomes, sometimes almost obsessively so. The danger is that we miss important relevance in the moment: we miss being present for those in our charge, and for their needs but we also distract ourselves from being present for us, too. We're less aware - let alone focused on our behaviours, thoughts, intentions, and choices. We become the leader on autopilot: a leader by title but not by behaviour. What I'm about to type will seem, as my father would say, "the bleedin' obvious", but very often the simplest things are the most memorable and powerful: to practice person-centred leadership we must focus on people. To change the outcome, we must change the process.

7
A Question of Leadership.

"You are today where your thoughts have brought you; you will be tomorrow where your thoughts take you."

James Allen

I ask a lot of questions and it is my belief that other people don't ask nearly enough. Questions are a simple yet highly effective pattern interrupt causing us to pause, and consider an answer to the question, which prompts us to reflect on both the current and alternative behaviour and/or consequent outcome. I am aware, and reminded relatively regularly, that asking a lot of questions might appear to be an irritating trait. Fortunately, you don't live with me.

However, something interesting happens in leadership with regards questioning, which I've observed over many years working individually with leaders at all levels, and in workshop and group contexts. Generally, most leaders seem to be good at asking of themselves questions that seek to better understand why things around them are happening, or their team are doing the things they are. However, these tend to be in the context of self-directed exasperation ("Why don't they just get on with it?"), and not necessarily directed to individuals, which would stimulate conversation, helping lead to resolutions. Bring inquisitive isn't only about efficiently discovering answers. Many of the questions I use help to positively challenge us, too. They help us grow and develop as leaders by better understanding people, situations and our own behaviours and ways of thinking. Without asking different questions, the many alternatives would not necessarily occur to us in isolation or without the prompt that questions provide. The idea of asking more questions may seem on face value overly simplistic, however, it is the very fact that we aren't asking enough questions as leaders, of ourselves or of those in our charge, that leadership frameworks become stale, distrusting, lack efficacy, and lead to some of the concerning statistics around leadership effectiveness we are seeing. Here's an example of some of the types of questions I ask when working with leaders to prompt nudges:

"What is the greatest challenge you currently face that would make the biggest difference to you/your team if it was solved?"

"If you don't have all the information you would like or require, what could you do with the information you do have? How can you sweat your assets?"

"What challenges do you foresee, and how will you plan to overcome them?"

"What happens in your job that makes you want to quit?"
This is my go-to question for appraisals and review meetings.

"What would make the greatest difference right now?"
Immediate focus and clarity can be immediately stress-relieving.

"What one thing this week could you have done differently that was within your control?"

Finding the right question to ask can be tricky, and if people don't know what to ask, they tend to do nothing. The correct first question to ask at any time is: "What is the right question to ask right now?". This seemingly simplistic question helps prompt and guide us to ask a question to get the process started, and closer to questions that will help challenge our thinking and help us grow.

In workshops with leaders, which are possibly some of my favourite pieces of work because of the rewarding journey we all go on during an intensive time together to explore and repair all manner of known and unknown issues, the questions I use are quite specific and intentional. They are designed to help nudge thinking, mindset, and behaviours and while they are tailored to each group and set of challenges, here's an insight into a recent workshop I ran with the country-wide leadership team of a global pharmaceutical company. You'll see how the questions help leaders to see and approach things differently, to feel about issues differently, and to better understand known and unknown issues.

There are always what I term 'Loud Problems', and 'Quiet Problems'. Loud Problems are like the obnoxious, loud five-year-old at a family party: everyone knows they are there, wishes they weren't, and can't help their attention be pulled toward them. Quiet Problems are not necessarily linked to Loud Problems, although they sometimes exist by association, but are over-shadowed by Loud Problems. These are the spilt drink on the carpet, the broken ornament, and the missing cat that no one notices because the five-year-old (the Loud Problem) commands our attention. Every organisation, and every individual within them, has Loud Problems and Quiet Problems. The loud ones are the ones I'm presented with and asked to help resolve and are often the ones I give the least time to because I know there are other problems that may be worse, or causal, but are unknown or overshadowed. Either way, they're not being given the attention they need for real change to happen.

I almost always begin any exercise by asking: "What isn't working?". It's an opportunity for everyone to vent, relax and feel safe. In my experience, it's the question most often avoided by my clients because of wanting to avoid the fallout. They don't want to handle the negativity, and fear the atmosphere will be tainted, instead wanting to keep things upbeat and positive. I understand their point of view, however, it's simply behavioural whitewashing. If you know there's something on someone's mind, address it first. If you don't, the pressing concern will remain a distraction for them, psychologically distancing them. Admittedly, encouraging and managing truthful feedback about what isn't working needs expert handling. What you're aiming to achieve is an atmosphere where people can calmly and objectively raise issues and concerns, and navigate to resolution, or at least understanding. Effective behavioral change is a constant dance of rupture and repair, but all too often the reality is rupture and avoidance. A healthy discussion about what isn't working and ways we may be able to repair or change those things sets us up for an honest, constructive session where people feel seen, heard, and valued. Within this first part of the session, finger pointing is often – but not always – external. It's equally important to ask what isn't working at leadership level in relation to efficacy, communication, vision etc.

To move forwards effectively, we must be able to do that together. For me, that begins by examining a behavioural framework everyone can measure themselves against, aspire to, and hold each other accountable for: "What are your organisation's values?" is the question that begins to expose some of the issues. Even at leadership level there's a degree of needing reassurance or confirmation from peers at what the organisation's values are, or even total cluelessness. How can you play the game if you don't know the rules? This is the first real wake-up call that there's more to address. Values change as the organisation does, and as the people in it do. Many values we carry as our core values for life, but our position on the things we find most important, or which we believe need more focus, will change over time. Organisational values are most effective when seen as a dynamic, living part of your DNA, not an expensive exercise to tick off a list once every ten years. I recommend you revisit them at least once a year, asking:

"Do these values represent us honestly right now?

Are they helping us?

Are there other values that are equally or more important to us right now?".

Once we have a grip of the wider values that are intended to guide the organisation, we can address something a little closer:

"What are my personal leadership values?".

All too often we consider the organisation's values as the only ones to exist but individual team values that support the wider company values are not only useful but essential. What happens at a local level day to day requires different values, and leaders should consider how they might adopt team-specific values that support their leadership style and aims. It's a beneficial exercise that can motivate and bring a team closer together. My personal preference is to use the organisation values as a starting point and add values for your team that sit under each, helping to reinforce or endorse.

When we're able to work together at all levels of an organisation, much of the friction extinguishes without the need for specialist intervention. Four of the most common issues that are aired during these workshops include:

1. Working in silos that results in blame, and general feeling of doom and gloom.
2. Poor communication.
3. Leaders feeling over-worked and with no time to lead.
4. Unclear on strategic direction.

Each of these is a result of a lack of presence and being too focused on the future. These issues become so big as to become a problem that impact efficacy, efficiency, motivation, well-being, and our ability to lead when the early signs are unseen because we're too distracted. People-centred leadership requires presence. It requires our attention, and it requires an effort to work together even when the draw to work in isolation is strong.

Adding the extension 'right now' to simple questions helps reframe them and keeps the context current. For example, "What do my team need *right now*?" is a question that never expires, and in my experience is not asked often, let alone often enough. If that question alone was asked more frequently, many resignations could be avoided as could negative silo working practices, time management issues, absence through stress, and many more issues leaders are required to oversee.

Asking questions challenges the status quo. If you hadn't already guessed, I have somewhat of an obsession with questions; specifically, the right questions that help create the most beneficial behavior changes. Of course, finding the right question is only part of the solution. For the question to be most effective, it must be asked at the right time. My first experience as to the power of questioning came back in 2011 when I began studying to become a coach. I wasn't at all comfortable with the seemingly cookie-cutter approach (some may argue 'classic') to coaching that was essentially a series of questions for the person coached to work everything out for themselves. My personal style has developed over the years to be much more of an advisor where I and the person I am coaching often meet in the middle to unpick the problem, combining their personal insight and my professional insight. I find it to be much more effective and well received than a persistent line of questioning. However, self-questioning is a powerful tool in the leadership arsenal, but many often stop short of getting to its ability to help make real changes when they don't like - or don't know - the answer to the questions they ask themselves. We are leaders in many more capacities than at work: as a parent, or dog owner, or even within the dynamics of a friendship group particularly when others are younger than us. Take, for example, a parent who makes what they begin to question to be the wrong decision when parenting their child. Perhaps, at their whit's end, tired and with a stubborn child refusing to do as they're told or acknowledge the respect their parent should be afforded, the parent smacked the child. The power struggle standoff was resolved, and the child sent to their bedroom crying. So many behavior choices were presented and made in such a short period of time, and with much emotion clouding clarity, that the parent now has time to reflect. Were those words the most appropriate to use? Were they fair? Does the way I handled that represent the parenting I hold true to my own values? Should I have smacked the child?

As the questions begin to be unpicked we are subject to confirmation bias, the halo effect and cognitive dissonance – all warping our reality and impacting our ability to learn. Despite this, we may, as we peer into the metaphorical mirror, see glimmers of the truth and it is how we respond to that truth – which could well cause us a degree of suffering – that determines how successful we are at responding to the questions we ask that have the potential to help us grow. If, as a result of seeing us for who we truly are, we are uncomfortable, we will lean into our confirmation bias and justify our actions. If the child hadn't push you so far, you would never have normally hit them. If you weren't quite so tired today, you wouldn't have snapped in the way you did. If they had just done as they were told, none of this would have happened. All excuses to remove the suffering and uncomfortable feeling the self-questioning has caused, giving us insight into where we could grow to become a better parent. As such, nothing changes. We might vow to never smack the child again, but what use is that vow when we have done little to work with the questions other than justify and shed the feeling of guilt and blame?

And so it is in boardrooms, offices, and remotely, up and down the leadership chain, from the very top to the most junior. Unless in a coaching or therapeutic environment, we tend not to ask sufficient questions, nor do we offer ourselves sufficient respect to provide time to reflect. I have no scientific or academic research to back this up, it is simply an educated guess – a hunch – but in much the same way that taking a short break from your desk to have a cup of tea, for example, can help lower stress levels, improve concentration, and help maintain productive output, taking time to self-reflect can help us achieve the same. All while getting us closer to the best version of ourselves.

If we don't know the right question to ask, we can begin by affording ourselves the right and self-respect to find the time for self-questioning with something as simple as: "Was that the right response? Could I have done anything differently, or better?". Sit with the answer, and as soon as there is a glimmer of something uncomfortable, we must have the resolve to stare at it face on. We are not defined by our behaviours. Making mistakes offers up the opportunity to grow, and a commitment to self if no one else, to pay it forward by improving in the future.

But if we never ask the question, we never further who we are.

8
With Leadership in Mind.

"Sometimes our light goes out but is blown into flame by another human being. Each of us owes deepest thanks to those who have rekindled this light."

Albert Schweitzer

I fear person-centred leadership may well become a corporate buzz-phrase, and a passing fad deemed a temporary distraction, much like NLP, and many of the fads littered through corporate history. As a leadership style that prioritizes treating people with care, respect, and benevolence, it deserves more time and serious study. It has much of the principle human tenets of Buddhism and Stoicism about it, which help create for the first time a formal structure, of sorts, to emphasise the importance of knowing those in our charge: understanding their strengths, weaknesses likes, dislikes. For practicing empathy and compassion, and creating meaning and purpose, not just to practice being the best version of ourselves, but to help build trust, loyalty, and productivity. With increased engagement, we see improved communication, and with that, organisational growth. Person-centred leadership is principally a mindset shift, but there are elements which can clearly help improve how we lead, not just how we think about it.

I've asked many leaders I've worked with, met, or interviewed what they believe the most successful qualities are for successful leadership. I recorded their responses for my own research into notebooks. Those notebooks contain conversations and responses from CEOs of global brands, senior Managing Directors, Vice Presidents etc, and have sat in my study for the best part of ten years. The responses vary in specifics according to their own personal experiences, however, what is especially interesting are the common themes; common threads that unify their experiences and opinions. When I spoke with Marshall Goldsmith, for example, he cited four common qualities of successful leaders:

Courage
Humility
Discipline, and
Adaptability.

There's much to be said for each of these qualities individually, but a word of caution. It can be overwhelming when many change examples are presented to us, leading to that awkward and deeply uncomfortable feeling of being so far from where you want to be. Almost as though the more we learn, the intrigue and excitement of our desire to improve draws us further from our point of reference. We focus on where we aren't, letting that overshadow all we have achieved, and the validity of where we are. For some, a particular one may stand out as something that would be especially useful to focus on right now. The reality is if they were each written on a piece of paper and plucked randomly from a bowl like a terribly disappointing tombola, they would likely have just the same impact. Focus on one for a set period; perhaps fourteen days, or a month, then focus on another, gradually working your way through the list and use them then to critically review your progress as a leader at the end of each quarter. Our work on these attributes is never over; it continues as we continue to lead and refine the craft. Actively and thoughtfully working on improving these core qualities will immeasurably improve your leadership style, ability, and efficacy.

Legal & General was established in 1836 and is one of the U.K.'s leading financial services groups and a major global investor. I've worked with them since 2016 and sat with their Managing Director of Retail Distribution in the U.K., Ali Crossley, to ask her thoughts about what makes an effective leader. She is hugely respected and valued by her team, and speaking from my own experience, a breath of fresh air to work alongside. Ali cares about people and the human condition, understanding the influence on both that comes with leadership.

Ali recalls readily and favourably several superiors in her career, but singled out Gary Shaughnessy, previous CEO of European Business at Zurich, and Ali's direct line lead when working together at Prudential, the Fortune 500 insurer. *"He stands out for me for continuing to be an amazing visionary and someone everyone wants to follow, whether in adversity or when doing well. He was inspirational because he taught me the importance of a level playing field in a meeting room. Until that point, I probably suffered more than I had consciously thought about from the authority gap that I think women are challenged by. He would make sure everyone in the room had a chance to speak, and he really listened, and really valued everyone's view. It felt so empowering. Being a leader is a huge privilege, as well as a huge responsibility. I remember leaving one of my jobs thinking 'I want to be a great leader, just how Gary was for me'. It makes such a difference. It can change people's careers and can change people's lives. It matters."*

I enjoy working with Ali. She really gets it. There's an authority owing to her experience, but a human vulnerability about her that is such a positive quality. Many believe vulnerability is a weakness, particularly in the field of leadership, however, Ali is one of those examples who demonstrates how being more human strengthens leadership. She is approachable, kind, wise, honest, sincere, and with an astute emotional intelligence rarer than it ought to be in leadership. When I asked Ali what she felt was required to be effective as a leader, she didn't hesitate: *"There are a few things. You need to be clear about your North Star: what you're trying to achieve and your direction. You don't necessarily have to go in a straight line to get there though and knowing you can go off course is important. You need to know you can go ultimately in the right direction by doing what is right for right now, knowing that it may well be off course slightly. It doesn't matter if you must detour or go off-piste, so to speak, providing you and your team are clear about where you are aiming for. Being clear about expectations around performance and commitment is important and having really high standards and setting a high bar for that. Probably the most important thing is being human: being approachable and accessible and democratic. I suppose being someone like Gary was to me. Making sure everyone feels valued and has an opportunity to have a voice. Recruit the very best people you can. I like to recruit people who are better than me; I'm not scared to do that; I think it's a fabulous thing. I can learn from them, and know they are the best person for the role to help us all achieve what together we are set to do. However, the very most important thing is to have vulnerability and the confidence to admit I don't have all the answers. Sometimes I get it wrong, and that's okay because I'm human like everyone else".* Ali makes it clear that it's not just one thing that makes an effective leader; it's a whole suite of techniques, focuses, and attributes that culminate in a well-rounded human experience where professionalism and emotional intelligence sit united, supporting each other.

I was especially interested to hear more of Ali's thoughts on vulnerability in leadership; something I've witnessed as being one of the cornerstones of effective leadership and a constant in high performing teams, yet commonly resisted for fear of perceived weakness or incompetence. How does she know when to share and when to withhold? Sometimes you may well have information that isn't appropriate to share, and other times you may not want to, but perhaps it would be beneficial. *"It's a judgement call. There are times when you may be desperate to share because you're feeling the pressure of something, but it isn't the right time to share because it's only selfish – it's not necessarily going to help anything, you just want to get it off your chest. I might be consumed by perhaps a financial decision I know is going to need to be made that may result in restructuring, for example, but sharing that isn't useful because people will only worry, and it may not even affect them. Conversely, there are times when I might be wrestling with which direction to go in when it's not clear, then I think it's great to have a conversation with several other people and get more views. You might still be no clearer as a result, but it's incredibly powerful to show vulnerability as a leader. None of us are invincible and more people than who care to admit have a degree of paranoia about imposter syndrome to some extent. Saying sorry is a powerful thing to do".*

Leadership isn't simply about having the knowhow to get from A to B, because that very rarely happens as intended. The details are rarely all there, the plan changes, and occasionally the result or destination changes, too. But Ali said something that was music to my ears. I've underlined it in my notebook. It was one of the most insightful – and human – responses I've heard and shows just how forward thinking and connected she is to her team, herself, and the concept of leadership as a craft. *"The greatest thing I've learned is that to retain the capacity and energy I need to keep going at the pace I need to, is to recognise the importance of fresh air. Specifically, for me I need fresh air, and exercise, and I have been clear with my own boss and team that if I don't get outside every day, I'm going to be grumpy. Feeling ground down and deenergised is not a good thing for a business. Do what is going to make a difference to your energy and your connectedness with feeling human; collect the children from school, get outside, go for a walk – whatever it is you need to do to help keep you grounded. Fortunately, businesses are generally much more tuned in to this sort of thing now, but I don't want my team to have to ask permission to get outside or get fresh air if that's what they need to do to work at their optimum."*

Allowing people to step out for fresh air, or connecting with nature, whether that be by simply having a desktop plant, or images of nature displayed on office walls, is not just "a nice thing to do", as one leadership graduate once dismissed it as to me. A growing body of research points to the beneficial effects that exposure to the natural world has on health, reducing stress and promoting health. I've been involved in this field since 2016 when I purchased a farm and began several research studies on the impact of nature on human health, wellbeing, and behavior. My team and I were one of the first to publish the beneficial results of having desktop plants in working environments. Studies now cite the positive effects of plants in working environments on happiness and productivity as anywhere from fifteen to forty percent. The last time serious research into how nature improved our health and mental wellbeing was in the 1970s. A few studies came along between then and now but really nothing that suggested this should be a field of serious study. I noticed that the 2019 global Covid-19 lockdown really changed that, with many more universities and research groups exploring the notion that nature might be good for us and setting out to prove why. Plentiful funding was made available and smaller nature and environmental charities dedicated funding to the subject, too, with the British Broadcasting Corporation (BBC) Gardener's World magazine publishing a 'Happiness Report' showing how much happier and satisfied with life gardeners were than non-gardeners. And yet, despite the evidence, some leaders I have worked with have made the decision to remove plants from their workspaces because people forgot to water them, or because they were "in the way". I make this point partly in the hope that you might add more plants into your workspace and to encourage people to engage with nature through outdoor meetings, a company garden, or staff room herb gardens, but also as a reminder to reflect on the decisions we make and why we make them.

Cian O'Brien has been the country head for several of the Volkswagen Group brands, including Audi of America and currently heads up Volkswagen Commercial Vehicles in the U.K. Don't tell him but he's in my top ten favourite clients. I know you shouldn't have favourites, but I do, and I've worked with Cian for almost ten years on various projects. His dedication to his team and continued development as a leader is admirable as another example of a leader who actively, consciously considers their leadership style and efficacy.

When I asked Cian about influential leaders in his own career, there were two examples that stood out for him: one from very recently, and one from the very start of his career. *"The current example would be Hildegard Wortmann, global sales, and marketing president for Audi but also responsible for a larger sales and marketing portfolio for Volkswagen Group. She was pivotal in changing organisational culture at Volkswagen Group. Hildegard has a lot of experience from different companies, in different countries and cultures. Prior to her arrival there existed a traditional linear leadership structure of top-down leadership, which Hildegard wanted to change, challenging an existing culture dominated by white, middle-class men to create a more unified approach where more people could contribute to the organisation's voice and culture. When she arrived, she wanted to put an end to the "yes" culture she inherited, putting everything on the table for consideration and change."*

This is a bold move few leaders have the courage to do when presented with an established environment structure that is dominating and overpowering in its traditional set up. It can be not only a daunting environment to walk into and function in, but the thought of the work involved to change that can be for some, overwhelming. What Cian is describing is a perfect model for leadership foundation in almost all cases: create an environment whereby everyone feels empowered, and safe enough to identify areas that don't work, or voice concerns. If change and improvements are accessible in the form of regular reviews, it helps prevent issues building up and going unidentified. Simultaneously it brings teams closer together, fostering a culture of trust, transparency, and teamwork, all of which vicariously encourage everyone to play a part in pursuing the best version of the organisation.

"Much earlier on in the start of my career during a short time in the naval defence in Ireland, a senior shore-based officer really made a lasting impression on me. Despite him being senior he was very keen to engage with troops. Whenever we returned from a sea trip, this senior officer would be there waiting to engage in conversation with all ranks. It was quite an alien experience compared to the traditional hierarchy on the ship and in our training; you just didn't interact with anyone that senior. One day while in conversation with him I asked why he was having these conversations, explaining how at odds they were to traditional rank hierarchy. He wanted to know what was happening from all perspectives, from all ranks, to help better inform his decisions and to know more accurately exactly what was going on.

It made me realise that you can have status and be in an elevated, senior position, but don't need to make people feel inferior or at a different level, which in turn prevents them from sharing things with you or approaching you."

Cian's experience is rare in some industries, but the approach is correct. The more connected we are as leaders, the more informed we are. Cian has a lot of experience with very different teams, in different countries, and in very different cultures. I was keen to see what his thoughts were on the essential characteristics of effective leaders.

"Authenticity. However, that's with a caveat and that's that you can be an authentic ass. It's crucial that people understand the real you. Everyone has strengths and weaknesses, and there will always be facets of both of those displayed so it's no use trying to hide them. If you don't have authenticity as a leader and you find yourself in a crisis and you suddenly display an alternative version of yourself, it can be both shocking and destabilising for your team. Openness

links to that, also because the engagement with your team is important. You want an environment where you all exchange your views, supporting a discussion that ensures a collective level of consideration in strategy and operation, for example. That openness helps you get the most from everyone. Then there's empathy. The ability to select a team, while understanding strengths and weaknesses of that team is a privilege. It's important to know and understand that some individuals might not work on their own but together as a team, they work well. It's a bit like being a conductor; the musicians each play a different instrument and your job is to bring those together in the right way to get the right harmony. I'd also say variance on perspective is critical. More perspectives are a good thing. I can be enthusiastic to get to a solution, but I've trained myself to listen and to pause to ask if anyone has any different ideas, or if anyone is thinking about something else. It changes the energy in meetings if you have the willingness to seek out and bring in those perspectives." Cian's point made me wonder:

How many of your team would have the confidence to challenge, or raise their own point of view?

If you haven't fostered a culture where individuals can share, how many ideas, or useful pieces of information, are you missing out on? There's a fine line between leadership and dictatorship, which depends on how much you are willing to listen. There is, however, a remarkable irony in that the very thing we as leaders look for and appreciate in those we lead, and which we feel is the most demonstrative of trustworthiness is when people ask for help. We want people to tell us when they don't know or need help. And yet it is the opposite for leaders themselves: it's the last thing most leaders will admit or demonstrate in themselves. I agree with this point Cian made: *"I think how we interact with members of our teams' needs be rethought. Those traditional top down, dictatorial methods of leadership are throttling.*

Self-awareness is a big deal for me. You need to have a high level of self-awareness about how people perceive you. My intention is never to intimidate people, but sometimes my energy and enthusiasm can come across as intimidating, and fostering an environment where people feel able to approach me has been useful for feedback because now I can contemplate how I'm presenting myself and ensure I'm not creating a level of disconnect because that can be disabling for both the team and the culture."

I asked Cian what the greatest lesson was he'd learned that helped inform how he leads today. *"At a point in my career I was very successful, being consistently promoted rapidly. When something like that happens, you find yourself in increasing positions of responsibility but can quickly discover your experiences aren't in line with the skillset required for some of those positions. The greatest lesson is in self-awareness and understanding your team: knowing the team strengths and weaknesses. Leadership is about adaptability. You can't just be a linear leader; you must adapt and evolve."* He's right, but self-awareness is impossible without vulnerability, and vulnerability isn't a characteristic that has been embraced in traditional leadership models. *"People will appreciate that much more when you're trying to inspire people, and to be honest about challenges or problems because people get behind you: no one wants to see someone willingly fail if they like you. That's what we're trying to get to: we want a successful organisation where we have people mirroring the behaviours leaders exhibit."* Cian and I are both fans of data-driven results and have had many discussions about the psychology of leadership and behavioural minutiae of high performance and leadership results. In a piece of research he was reading, Cian shared a study he had discovered looking into honesty in leadership, which asked: *How do you perceive the willingness of leaders that would admit they don't know the answer?* The answer was a single digit percentage of leaders who would admit they didn't know the answer to something. Why is honesty and vulnerability seen as a weakness among so many leaders? It's a much safer position for any organisation to be in when led by honesty and integrity. We wouldn't stand for it in those we lead, so what exactly are we hiding? Somewhat ironically, authenticity seems to be the latest leadership buzz word, but how do you be authentic? It's a difficult concept for some to understand.

The misconception is that being authentic at work begins with having the confidence to be ourselves at work. However, the first step really is in knowing ourselves. We are different people at work to whom we are at home, and that, for me, is where the problem begins. Perhaps the difference between who we are at home and at work is, to a degree, irrelevant because we are still a human: we still have the same core needs. The notion of bringing your best self to work suggests that we should be leaving certain parts of us at home, but which parts? The more human parts? Compassion, our core emotional needs, and vulnerability? Being authentic is about who you are. Workplace or at home, to be authentic is to be us. We are many things as humans: storywriters, story tellers, change makers, innovators, loved, loving, angry, lonely, bright, insecure, intelligent, curious, agile, emotional, complicated, over-thinkers, vulnerable, courageous, resilient, passionate, perfectly imperfect. We are a combination of information and experiences of everything we have ever learned; of books read, and people we have loved. Workplaces need to become more supportive environments for humans. Somewhat ironically, many leaders I work with don't feel they had sufficient training to be a leader, but it is commonly encouraged in the workplace to be authentic. If your vulnerability is that you feel you don't have the answers, or sufficient knowledge or experience to lead as you feel you should, the advice to be authentic – and therefore, vulnerable – is the very advice you will reject and act against for fear of losing your job or appearing weak. The people we are afraid of – our senior bosses or decision makers, or colleagues we look to for validation and acceptance – have fears, too. The best value a leader can bring is their authenticity to be able to say: "I don't have all the answers. What do you all believe we should do?". Vulnerability connects all of us because it is entirely relatable, and we can only become more authentic if we allow ourselves to be more vulnerable. Yet

I coached the Chief Operating Officer of a recognisable global brand, which, for reasons that will become apparent, I won't share here to protect their identity. After about a year, they asked to speak to me out of our regular scheduled sessions about something that was proving difficult for them. An impending restructure of the organisation meant that they had been invited to become the company CEO. With that promotion came a significant pay rise and many benefits, and the requirement for an extra-long day every Tuesday. An early start and late finish owing to reports and meetings that for technical, legacy, and structural reasons were fixed weekly on that day. I sensed there was a conflict but everything I had heard so far sounded, professionally at least, positive. "But I don't think I can do it", came my client's response. "They've only offered it to me, despite many others wanting the job, but I take my son swimming on a Tuesday. He has autism, and the routine is important, but there are no other lessons we can go to. Besides, that's my time – it's our time." And so, they turned the job down. The company attempted to convince them to take the job, at one point even increasing the salary bonuses offered believing they could attract my client with – genuinely impressive - financial incentives. However, my client's vulnerability was being true to themselves, and I've never stopped talking about them, or respecting them for an act of total commitment to being true. Authenticity is rarely without sacrifice. I spent a long time reflecting on my client's conundrum and tying to answer this simple question: Why do we expect people to be less human?

You don't necessarily have to agree with people but seeking to understand them is the cornerstone of empathy: seek to obtain as much information as possible to help you make the most effective decisions. Cian is keen to bring his team close to his decision making and understand the value in doing so: *"Psychological safety is a prerequisite to deliver innovations in this industry as we spend much consideration on transformation: electrification, digitisation, the customer journey etc. Psychological safety is the willingness of participants to take personal risks in an environment where there is the potential for that to happen. I think leaders, whether that's an SME with a single leader or huge organisations, must acknowledge the most important part of a leadership role is to generate high levels of psychological safety to ensure we're not running into an Emperor's Clothes scenario. It begins by taking time to understand the perspective of those in your team and indeed the wider organisation: "How am I perceived? How do they experience me in interactions? My personal ambition is to reduce hierarchy. I want to create a special forces unit or sports team where everyone has an opportunity to present their view; to challenge if they don't understand something. Enabling psychological safety brings much more results much quicker."*

I asked Cian what a safe environment looks like for him. His response was clear and profound: *"human-centred leadership"*.

9
Reflections.

"I hope you know you are capable, brave, and significant – even when it feels like you are not."

Mel Robbins

I have been working in the field of leadership in various capacities directly and indirectly, for twenty-one years. Certainly, in the last five years my work has focused more on behaviour and the craft of leadership. In that time, I've worked with new and aspiring leaders, and senior leaders of some of the world's largest organisations helping solve a remarkably diverse range of problems by helping uncover questions to ask that help change behaviours. I'm not one to look back and hadn't truly appreciated that I have seen a lot of people, a lot of problems, and a lot of organisations throughout my career. When it was brought to my attention that I had been working in this field for twenty-one years it prompted a lot of reflection, caused mostly because it came as a complete surprise to me. Where had those twenty-one years go? And what of the next twenty-one?

What have I learnt about leadership in that time? Principally that there are a lot of things people don't tell you, most likely because they don't know. For so long now, much of leadership has been about formulaic systems and structures, created by people who I can only imagine have not been leaders. Or not especially good ones. In England, the interference of leadership with no clinical experience into the running and decision-making of the National Health Service has contributed to the resulting destruction of one of the world's flagship health systems, such is the detrimental impact of people with opinions about things they know nothing about overseeing those very things. As Donald Rumsfeld famously asserted, "there are unknown unknowns", and oh! to be blissfully ignorant! A shiny new system offering so much promise to leadership: how attractive that must have seemed. Indeed, it continues to be for so many that following this system, or buying into that process, will create a fully functioning leadership team. However, these out of the box style frameworks overlook the most important element of leaders: the people doing the leading. Those creating the attractive looking solutions have not led. They have not, as Theodore Roosevelt dramatically put it, been "marred by dust and sweat". One of the most important things people don't ever tell you is that leadership is hard work. It's difficult, it's dynamic, and requires constant attention to hone and develop the skills required for it to be successful – and it requires a significant level of self-reflection. Leadership is a journey on which real change happens. However, I'm not sure seeing it as a destination or an achievable competency outcome, is useful. We must work at it throughout our careers. Some of the best leaders I have had the privilege of working with are especially good reflectors; they have developed an ability to readily pause and reflect on their actions, consciously considering where they may have done something differently or how they may learn something that could positively impact future behaviours. I remember when I first began meditating and how easily distracted I was, my mind wandering to other thoughts. But how I'd suddenly become conscious of having not meditated for several days: it takes time for new behaviours to become habits, and that begins by catching ourselves not doing the things we want to do more frequently. Leadership is no different. In fact, the most common characteristic of effective, impressionable leaders is not that they put their team first but that they consider their team as one with themselves: truly one team. This is only possible, however, when we have first spent time working on ourselves as leaders to better understand and improve our core human skills like emotional intelligence, empathy, and kindness, and to really get to know ourselves through our personal values, boundaries, and deep inner meaning. There are a lot of individuals in leadership positions getting by, seemingly getting away with it. Likely not without a heavy dose of imposter syndrome. If we understand the value of a team who respects us as a formative leader, and as a result will be more open to working with us not simply for us, it should be encouragement enough to put the work in. Like much in life, we have a choice. Much is within our control:

whether we have the courage to show up authentically, or if we adopt a personality seeking validation based on how we believe others wish us to show up. To be more mindful and present, or to charge through life. To choose to find meaning in life at work and at home, or to allow time to simply tick away. To actively choose to be a better leader, or to spend a career dealing with consequences. The choice is ours. The choice is yours.

Despite the choice, many leaders are heavily influenced by the leadership character they believe they should adopt, and it is this influence which so often overshadows the ability to be authentic. The title brings with it a heady mix of assumptive control and the need to be someone different, yet the reality could not be further from the truth. Leadership does not dictate, demand, or desire us to be different people; simply to learn new skills. If I've learnt one thing over anything else in the last two decades working in the field of leadership, it's that there is an inauthenticity pandemic. The need to act up is a plague on leadership efficacy that rots trust, respect, and all but destroys genuine human-centred leadership. With hindsight, I have been remarkably privileged to have coached so many leaders and been offered an insight into the thinking, insecurities, and complexities of becoming and being a leader. At its heart is the challenge many leaders have in showing vulnerability, which is the cornerstone of authenticity. What is somewhat ironic, and troubling, is that it is the very characteristic leaders extol in those they lead. I've come to learn largely the only thing preventing leaders from willingly showing vulnerability is fear; the fear they will appear weak, unsure, or incompetent owing to any glimmer of not being infallible. This isn't The Hunger Games – leadership is simply human beings leading human beings. We must change this toxic rhetoric. When I do see partial vulnerability it is supported by trust: a trusting environment in which they work, with support from colleagues and superiors. And when we talk about vulnerability, I'm not suggesting we must not have any boundaries, or sense of personal space, or to be entirely emotionally loose; it is perfectly possible to be strong and vulnerable.

The word vulnerable comes from the Latin *vulnus*, meaning wound. From there it becomes *vulnerare*, meaning to wound, then late Latin *vulnerabilis,* and eventually in the early seventeenth century it became the word vulnerable. The very meaning and legacy of the word throughout all of history suggests weakness. A wounded person or animal is less able to successfully fight to their victory; their health and survival compromised by less natural protection. We talk about the elderly being vulnerable members of our society; of young children being vulnerable, especially in perilous environments, and of sick and injured animals being vulnerable to disease and predation. Historically, to be vulnerable is hardly an aspiration. It is only very recently in the late twenty-first century that the notion of being vulnerable has become to be seen as something of a positive character quality. There was a time in our species history when it was advantageous to be perceived as strong, regardless of the reality: to cover up how we really felt. Likewise, there was a time in history when it wasn't considered necessary to wash our hands before performing surgery. And look where both of those behaviors got us. We are all vulnerable; there are no human exceptions. It is time we began to normalise the notion of being more human and demonstrating truly human qualities, if for no other reason than to show others – who all feel the same range of emotions – that we are just like them, and vicariously that we understand them. Owing to this, leaders who show vulnerability are able to create psychologically safe working environments because employees are more comfortable being more themselves, too, and we know that, in turn, this relaxed psychological state leads to more creative risk-taking, sharing of perspectives, and valuable contributions. We can all recall at time when we held back a suggestion or opinion for fear of how others may perceive us. I often wonder how many wonderful ideas have been lost and wasted this way.

In the same way our views on washing hands, cleaning teeth, and disposing waste into the ocean have all changed, I would suggest that our view of vulnerability is beginning to change in popular culture, but there still much resistance in the field of leadership. It is a strength, not a weakness. It shows an emotionally intelligent and connected person who is able to look inwardly and be present with being human. It demonstrates someone who is able to connect more readily to others, and who likely possesses greater joy, creativity, and love. It is an essential part of being human, and evermore an essential part of an efficacious leader.

10
To Know Our Worth.

"Be tolerant with others and strict with yourself."

Marcus Aurelius

One of the great honours, and indeed joys of my work, is having personal, one to one time with leaders around the world in the form of coaching and advisory work. In confidence, these sessions often see deep vulnerability shared unseen in any other forum. Discussions vary wildly from the deeply personal to the entirely professional, and often a unity of the two. We rarely leave what happens at home there, and neither do we remain unaffected by our work so much that it doesn't creep into our home life. It remains a sincere privilege to hold a space where others feel comfortable enough to discuss the things most affecting or important to them entrusting me to help guide them to a resolution.

Marlon is the Vice President of a company with offices in nine countries and we were six months or so into our coaching journey together when we began discussing whether I might do some wider work with more of his team. Marlon introduced me to his colleague in the training department, and we discussed the scope of work and fee. Unfortunately, the budget wasn't available, and we agreed to pick up the project again later in the year when into the new financial year. When I next spoke with Marlon, he mentioned that his colleague had told him they were unable to make it happen but that they were impressed with the way I handled the issue with budget. Marlon was unaware of the exact details of our conversation, and asked how I priced my services, and how I knew what to charge. I explained that I know my worth and of the value my work brings. Marlon went quiet, and reflecting, asked me: "I don't think I know my worth. How do you know?".

It was the first time I'd heard anyone admit that. I will tell you what I told him.

It is a question of self-esteem. How do we value what we do? Not in financial or commercial terms, but in the context of life, purpose, and meaning? This isn't an exercise about justifying a raise in salary, but of contribution. It is an exercise of self-validation of meaning of human value. The more interesting and useful question is not "how do I know my own worth?", but "why do I not know my own worth?". For many, the notion of their awareness of self-worth is contingent upon external validation and external factors. We will feel successful and deem ourselves to be a success if we earn a specific amount of money, or are bestowed a particular title, or drive a certain car. Perhaps if we achieve a weight loss goal, we will feel we are worthy of attention, or a sense of achievement. For many that realisation of self-worth is based on the number of likes their social media posts get or how many followers they have - or how many matches they receive on a dating app. When our sense of worthiness is reliant on external factors, we have little control over how we feel. We place the control of how we feel about ourselves entirely in the hands of others, and it is this toxic situation – a toxic choice, most commonly centring around appearance and approval – that is worse for our self-esteem.

It began for me by listening to positive feedback and testimonials, which I used to always ignore because they made me feel uncomfortable. It was a mix of disbelief and, in hindsight, imposter syndrome, as if the feedback was offered from a time when I delivered something good by fluke. I rationalised after a while that, with so many positive messages that were sometimes so remarkably generous in their praise, perhaps there was a grain of truth in what these people were saying. Perhaps – perhaps – I should listen to them. These positive affirmations from others helped me accept where my strengths were. While I still find it a little uncomfortable to receive praise, there is a fine line between knowing what we are good at, and arrogance, and if navigated carefully we can identify those things we are good at, and what we bring that some others do not. Each of us has unique qualities, ideas, or experiences, and when we know them, we can begin to accept and hone them. Hearing them from others is not part of a contingent acceptance; it is merely a way to confirm what we may not know ourselves – it helps answer the most pressing question: Who am I? Reducing external contingencies is always a healthier option because the reliance on others and not self, leads us to another toxic space of dopamine chasing and a distorted sense of who we are. Getting to know why you do what you do, and what makes you good at it can mean leaning into an extremely vulnerable space, especially if it results in the realisation that where we thought our strengths were, others do not. That is a powerful space for growth, however, and I spend a lot of time reflecting and spotting opportunities for growth in everything I do from projects to specific work tasks, to conversations and relationships: if anything doesn't go as intended, or fails, it can be seen as a great opportunity to improve, develop, and grow.

It becomes inherently difficult to feel worthy or to be clear about your worth if you experience imposter syndrome. Some studies suggest as many as eighty percent of us experience it at some point in their lives, but where did imposter syndrome come from? Pauline Clance is the famed psychologist who first put a name to imposter syndrome back in 1978 in a paper she co-authored with Suzanne Imes: 'The Imposter Phenomenon in High Achieving Women'.

The paper describes it as "an internal experience of intellectual phoniness". As a Financial Times magazine interview with Clance describes: "Imposter are ambitious, hard-working people who believe they must have fooled anyone who thinks that they are capable or talented." If it's a feeling that sounds familiar to you, you are in good company. Lauded physicist Albert Einstein once remarked: "The exaggerated esteem in which my lifework is held makes me very ill at ease. I feel compelled to think of myself as an involuntary swindler." Even Maya Angelou, Nobel laureate and author admitted: "I have written eleven books, but each time I think 'Uh oh, they're going to find out now.'" The fears, Clance explains from personal experience, transcend age, education, or factual proof of the opposite.

Technically, imposter syndrome isn't a "syndrome"; a clinical term for a malady that must feature the "four Ds" of mental illness (deviance, distress, dysfunction, and danger) as dictated by the DSM (Diagnostic and Statistical Manual of Mental Disorders). Clance herself originally referred to it as a phenomenon but says "syndrome" became so popular that she gave up trying to correct people.

For a long time now, the imposter phenomenon has been associated particularly with professional women. Sophie Turner is a professional coach and founder of 'Yes She Can', an equality collective focused on creating a community for women and allies to change how women are seen in the workplace. Sophie believes it's something we must learn to manage: "In my experience it never goes away. What we try to do is minimise the internalised voice that imposter syndrome has and work on never allowing that voice to impact our decisions and therefore our successes and career progression."

I asked Sophie what do we do about that voice because the self-doubting critic can be toxic and debilitating – does managing it really work? After all, what if the voice is right and you are an imposter? Would that be an indication that you're outside of your comfort zone, perhaps? Sophie points out that this level of realisation is important and helps individuals to determine if what they are sensing is imposter syndrome, or indeed something else. "If you were to say here are my strengths and here are my weaknesses, that self-discovery is important because it demonstrates a level of self-awareness. If as part of that there's a realisation that I'm not wholly comfortable and my skills or experience aren't right for the task I'm doing or the position I'm in, I'm able to do something about it." I'm interested to know what Sophie thinks the differences are between imposter syndrome and the feeling of being outside of our comfort zone. "We are lifelong learners, but we've been made to feel that we're not allowed to be outside of our comfort zone. That feeling, of having overstepped our comfort zones is when we feel like we haven't done something before and don't know how it's going to go. The imposter syndrome feeling is broader than that; it's us feeling like we're impacted by informal structures and feeling like we don't belong, which ultimately is a hindrance to our sense of belonging and lifelong learning. It all comes down to external pressures. The golden thread is that feeling of a lack of self-worth and self-confidence born out of family and society pressures, and expectations of both. Fortunately, organisations can do very simple things to help prevent imposter syndrome prevailing by providing regular qualitative and quantitative feedback on whether individuals are good enough at their job."

I mention to Sophie that imposter syndrome was born from something that Clance identified especially in professional women, and why she thought that might be. "Imposter syndrome really impacts any minority group more. As a minority, whether that's as a woman in a male-dominated industry, or a person of colour in an overly white environment, or as a younger member of a team among older colleagues, you don't fit the immediate environmental norm. You look different, or are different and if you don't fit the mould you are having to adapt to fit in."

I wonder if feeling a degree of imposter syndrome is normal? Is it us feeling out of our comfort zone and essential for us all to feel at some point? "Very possibly", Sophie says. "By labelling the experience it helps us to understand what the individual is encountering. From an organisation perspective, however, it often gets used as an excuse." I ask Sophie what she means, and I begin to recall times when I've seen this first hand with organisations I've advised. "The term imposter syndrome has been bandied about so often and loosely now that organisations are using it as an excuse for not inherently changing their approach towards women and minority groups."

Clance has her own advice for those who experience imposter feelings: "Remember a success you've had. Then invite your boss in the room. What would they say? Then let someone else in, maybe your professor. Then the head of the project. Then your father, your sister. What would they say? Observe their conversation. Once the room is full, I ask you... don't you think it's interesting that you can fool so many bright people?".

Sometimes the brightest of people we fool, are ourselves.

11

The Value of Values.

"If your actions create a legacy that inspires others to dream more, learn more, do more, and become more, then you are an excellent leader."

Dolly Parton

I attended a relatively small secondary school in rural Buckinghamshire, England and really enjoyed my time at school. I visited it several years after leaving and it's different now. I think I was fortunate to enjoy a very special period in that school's history, a unique mixture of teaching talent, timing, opportunity, support, and progress in a small, friendly village school. In many ways, retrospectively, it was idyllic. I know I'm fortunate – so many have painful stories of their time at school. I had unique relationships with many of the teaching staff, often spending extra-curricular hours at school and on field trips or seeing them outside of school in the local area, and as such became friendly with many of them. One teacher, Mr. Jeremy Davies, taught German and was the school's PSHE lead (appointed to help guide staff and students in personal, social, health and economic issues), later to become PSHRE and include religion. He taught me German, and was by virtue of me being a student, responsible for ensuring I had PSHE support. I often passed him cycling to or from school as I walked home. He had a fantastic sense of humour that I'd describe as 'Pythonesque', and I know he was a fan of Monty Python. Fun, gentle, kind, compassionate and unafraid to show his humanity, he was a wonderful human, and a lovely man.

On February 3rd, 2016, Jeremy Davies died. Several students, and many of his peers and colleagues attended his funeral along with his wife, two young daughters, and friends and family. So well attended was the service that many of us had to stand at the back of the room. It was a moving service, made especially more so given how young he was and the purity of his humanity. It is an overused sentiment, but the world really did lose one of its brightest lights that day. A beautiful and unexpected gift was given to those who attended; a compact disc containing some of Jeremy's favourite songs he had personally selected. On the cover is an image of him that he also chose, peacefully looking to the camera on a river boat. Every time I hear the songs 'Moonshadow', or 'Underneath the Stars', I think fondly of Jeremy Davies and the gentle impact he made on me, and no doubt many others. He is one of the reasons I know and trust authenticity as a useful method for modelling behaviour, and an inspiration for leading from the heart.

Jeremy's professional motto he used at school, and likely his personal one, too, was profoundly simple, and one I have since adopted for my own life in my work and at home:

Dignity, love, respect.

Three deceptively simple words that help guide, remind, inform, and nurture. They are the founding principles I offer to all organisations when working with them on culture or leadership programs. Interestingly, most choose to replace the word love. At first, I struggled with this; I didn't like that it was being replaced. I still don't wholly agree with it. Some replace with the word compassion, which is a fair compromise, and others with corporate words that really aren't a useful replacement for something so human at all, such as: liking, friendliness, together. However, if Jeremy's legacy inspires people to explore creating their moral compass, then I guess his legacy is a success, regardless of the specific words they adopt. What I've come to learn is that many of my clients, whether individuals or organisations, fear using the word love. They're scared of the consequences of using one of the most powerfully emotive words in the English language. Yet, if we spoke more literally in a way that was easier for people to understand, and indeed if the world had more love and actions of compassion towards one another, we would be closer to peace. And by virtue, further from hatred, stress, and war. I can't help but feel a little sad when people feel the need to hide part of themselves. Even more so when we vicariously encourage it through actions at work.

Many leaders, parents, teachers, sales professionals, and individuals I work with have yet to understand their worth. Very few have considered their own values, and the two are intricately linked. As such, they find themselves in a position where their personal boundaries are frequently compromised leaving them anxious, angry, or resentful but without knowing why. Most of us can offer things that may help define our values: a dislike for racism, violence, or obnoxious people, for example. You may inherently know you dislike selfish people, or those who aren't team players, or who are tyrannical. We learn the things we like and dislike through experiences and reflection, but what about our core values?

What do we stand for?

What do we willingly accept to be right, and wrong?

What do we strive for?

What do we categorically not accept in ourselves or others?

What do we try to avoid in ourselves?

What are we happy to compromise on, or not?

What triggers us or makes us feel uncomfortable – and what do we do about it?

Perhaps most importantly, how do those values show up in our every day?

As you read these questions you may experience a sense of familiarity; these are constructs you know exist and questions or propositions you may have heard before. However, if I were to ask you to put pen to paper and answer them fully for me now, would you be able to do that? Try it - you'll see for yourself what happens when I run workshops on leadership and organisational values: we discover that what looks simple on face value is quite a bit more difficult than we realise. More difficult than we would like to admit, perhaps. Understanding something is different to knowing it.

What the exercise reveals is that we are leading blindly, entirely unable to be clear about, and therefore be mindful of, the most important part of being human: our values. And without values we can't get close to understanding our worth.

Some clients will declare their values with well-meaning and inspiring words like "trust"; "service"; "delivering value"; "leading with integrity". However, those words need clear explanation and deep understanding to bring them alive. What does "trust" look like when you are writing an email? How do you demonstrate "leading with integrity" on the telephone with a customer? What does "quality" look like when in a team meeting? We can't live values we can't name or understand. Leaving it to instinct, or even worse imagination, only results in inconsistency, confusion, and disparity. Our values need much more consideration to know what they look like and what the parameters are, for ourselves and for others living them, too.

In the ever-evolving landscape of leadership as a craft and serious field of study, the significance of values has emerged as a cornerstone of effective leadership. Values serve as the bedrock upon which organizations build their cultures, guide their decisions, and shape their futures. They act as a compass that directs leaders through the complexities of their roles, providing clarity and consistency in action. Understanding the critical importance of values enables leaders to inspire trust, foster engagement, and create environments that thrive on collaboration and innovation. They are more than simply a tick-box exercise, which is how many I have worked with have approached them.

At their core, values are deeply held beliefs about what is important. They guide behaviors and decisions, acting as a moral compass in both personal and professional realms – and that's why we need to also explore personal values, not simply the professional ones of our organisations. Values often encompass a wide array of concepts, including integrity, respect, innovation, collaboration, and accountability. But in the context of leadership, values not only serve as a personal guide but also as a collective framework that, if chosen well, can unite both local teams and entire organizations. They create a shared understanding of what is acceptable and expected, fostering a sense of belonging and purpose among team members. There is good reason why almost all my work begins with values: the role of values in leadership can be complex and is multifaceted. Of course, they help leaders clarify their vision and mission. A leader who understands their values can articulate a compelling vision that resonates with others and which in turn inspires, engages, and motivates teams, driving engagement and commitment. But values also influence decision-making. In the face of challenges or ethical dilemmas, leaders with a strong value system are better equipped to navigate difficult choices, relying on their values to guide their decisions, and ensuring consistency and integrity in their actions. Values are the stories we tell ourselves; how we live them defines us. They shape organizational culture, but it is leaders who set the tone for how values are perceived and practiced within their organizations. Strong cultures that are rooted in shared values enjoy enhanced collaboration, increased morale, and overall improvements in performance. They are a critical part of the DNA of the organisations we lead, but of us, too.

There are many benefits to values-driven leadership, but one of the most significant is the trust it fosters. When leaders are seen to consistently demonstrate their values, we create an environment where those in our charge feel safe and valued because leaders who embody their values are much more likely to gain the respect and loyalty of their teams. Employees want - and I'd argue need - to follow leaders who are authentic, transparent, and principled. But those are personality traits that require our focus and take work. However, when we prioritize our values, we enhance our credibility and inspire others to act with integrity, too. There are commercial benefits to incorporating values into our wider model of work, too: they play a crucial role in employee engagement. When employees understand and connect with the values of their organization, we see greater engagement and commitment to their work. One of the frequent challenges organisations face, is how to consistently engage employees to maintain motivation, productivity, and encourage them to go above and beyond in their roles. It's a challenge that is largely resolved by living values which in turn helps foster a sense of belonging. It's no secret that employees who feel aligned with their organization's values are more likely to be satisfied with their jobs and remain with the organization long-term, with research consistently demonstrating that organizations with strong values outperform those that lack them. One of the most interesting parts, for me, of working with high-performing individuals is the pattern of them seeking workplaces or teams where their own values align with those of the organization.

Often it's organisational values that are the first step but before leaders can effectively instil values within their organizations, they must first define their own values.

What qualities do I admire in others?

What experiences have shaped my beliefs?

How do I define success, both personally and professionally?

I'd encourage you to enhance your authenticity and refine it in your answers, for if we can act in alignment with our values, we will inspire others to do the same. That's not to say that organisational values should be devised, defined, and dictated by leaders. If values are the rules we're all going to play by, and the guidelines we will live by – at work at least – then stakeholders, employees, customers, and partners can provide valuable insights, and in my book should be encouraged to do so. Collate that information how you see fit, whether it's by conducting surveys, chairing focus groups, or facilitating informal workshops but don't take the easy route of simply generating inspiring sounding words that look impressive when printed in large vinyl graphics on a wall. You'll miss the opportunity to gather important perspectives on what values resonate most within the organization for internal and external stakeholders – all those who will be impacted by them. When stakeholders are involved in defining values, they are more likely to embrace and uphold them.

As I've alluded to already, once values are defined, the next step is to articulate them in a clear and compelling manner. This is the step the majority of clients I work with fail to do well, if ever at all. What do the values look like in terms of behaviors, in the context of how the organisation functions?

In leadership we are being watched, all the time. When we demonstrate our values in action, we set a precedent for others to follow. I've often said that leadership is not dissimilar to being an actor: there's a need to be present all the time, and when this isn't authentic, it can be exhausting. It becomes quite literally an act. Being present requires intentionality and consistency. An added benefit of regularly reflecting on our actions and decisions, asking ourselves whether they align with the stated values, is that it keeps us mindful. It prevents us from leading on autopilot, blindly unaware. A leader who is visibly committed to their values creates a culture where others feel empowered to do the same: we are being watched, all the time.
To reinforce values within an organization, it is leaders who must actively recognize and reward behaviors that align with those values. While peer to peer recognition is valuable, it is the leadership recognition that helps specifically enforce values by modelling, whether that be formal recognition programs or informal praise during team meetings. Celebrating values-based achievements not only reinforces the importance of those values but motivates others to embrace them, too. When employees see their peers being recognized for embodying organizational values, they are more likely to follow suit, such is the power of behavioral modelling: we want to fit in and feel as though we belong to a united effort.

For values to truly permeate an organization and its culture, however, they must be integrated into policies, practices, and performance evaluations. This means ensuring that recruitment, onboarding, training, and performance management all reflect the organization's values. And it is here where most I have experienced are let down. During the hiring process, for example, leaders should assess candidates not only for skills and experience but also for alignment with organizational values. Will this person fit? Much more priority needs to be given to whether candidates complement organisational values because if they don't, they certainly cannot be held responsible. Yet rarely are values discussed during interview or onboarding, and when they are they are presented in such a way that leaves plentiful room for interpretation. If we are to make a difference immediately with our values, performance evaluations should include criteria that assess how well employees embody the organization's values in their work. A rudimentary example of this would be to use the values as a checklist and together consider each one, offering examples of how the individual embodies the values: how often do they demonstrate them and to what extent?

Leaders must lean on their values to guide their decision-making and maintain integrity but can only do so when those values exist as more than simply words on a wall or displayed on a presentation from HR. You either live values or you don't. If you don't, it has to be questioned whether there is any point in having the values in the first place. It is the leaders who prioritize their values who emerge stronger and more respected, and by making decisions that align with their values, leaders build trust and credibility, even in challenging times. Values first, always.

However, having said that, it can at times be far from simple or straightforward to do so, especially when leaders encounter situations where their values conflict with the interests of the organization or stakeholders. Navigating these conflicts requires careful consideration and transparency. It requires honesty and vulnerability. It requires emotional intelligence and human-centred leadership. When I received a call back in 2021 quite unexpectedly from the Vice President of a company I had run a leadership workshop for, I knew something wasn't right. They cut straight to the point: they were staring right in the face of a quite significant values conflict with their board. Several non-executive directors were suggesting something that did not sit well with my client, and to make matters worse, the organisation's executive committee were making similar suggestions. My client, in her words, wanted "to avoid any confrontation at all costs". The issue with that position is in defining confrontation. To confront the matter head on is precisely what we need to do and engage in open dialogue with stakeholders, seeking to understand different perspectives. That does not mean to say it will be punitive, or aggressive, or confrontational. We must seek to understand. By prioritizing values, the very values both committees signed off, and facilitating conversations around them, my client was able to find solutions that honoured their principles, whilst simultaneously addressing the needs of the organization. It is to be expected that as organizations grow and adapt, their values may need to evolve. It's an important and fundamental characteristic common of leading high performing teams that values are reassessed and updated as part of a regular schedule in response to changing circumstances or feedback from stakeholders. Regardless of whether your aim is to become high performing, it's essential that we ensure the values we uphold are relevant to the people we lead and the work they do. People change, cultures change, and values must, too.

The influence of values extends beyond immediate effects on performance and culture; they shape the long-term legacy of a leader. As discussed elsewhere, leaders who prioritize and embody their values leave an indelible mark on their organizations and the people they serve. A strong legacy rooted in values can inspire future generations of leaders. But building a values-driven organization is not a one-time effort; it is an ongoing commitment that requires leaders to continually assess and reinforce values. When you put values – the signposts for our behaviors – at the centre of your organization, you create a values-driven organization which fosters a culture of accountability, innovation, and engagement. This creates an environment where those we lead become champions of the values, driving the organization forward with purpose and passion.

In a world where change is the only constant, the importance of values in leadership remains unwavering. Values are not merely abstract concepts; they are the guiding principles that shape decisions, actions, and cultures. Leaders who recognize the power of values and commit to embodying them can transform their organizations by building trust, enhancing engagement, and driving performance. Values-driven leadership is human-centred leadership, and it creates a sustainable and thriving workplace.

When I work away from home, if there is opportunity to, I like to explore the local area. Mainly because I love to walk and it's a great opportunity to get out of a confined hotel or conference venue to get my daily dose of fresh air and nature. In a shop in rural England, I saw a large wooden sign for sale; the kind used for decorative accents normally with a quippy or gimmicky saying on them. On this were printed "family values", and they read:

"Our Family Values:
Integrity: we do what we say. We are the same inside and outside the front door.
Radical Honesty: anything that is hidden is brought into the light.
Courage: we are bold to speak hope, truth, and life; speech over silence.
Loyalty: we send each other out and always have each other's back.
Laughter: laughter and praise are the echo of our home.
Vulnerability: we share our joys, sorrows, and ourselves with each other.
Wholehearted: we are worthy of each other's love, and we live without fear."

I particularly liked "speech over silence". Poor communication is often the cause of deep ruptures, unresolvable if left unrepaired. Sadly, many organisations I work with have less values than appeared on this sign, and often without the fuller explanation. It's a good point of inspiration though, which is why I've included it here, and I hope it helps prompt thinking, reflection, and discussions at home and at work. It isn't fair to punish people if they don't know the rules.

Our values are our greatest asset. Embrace them, champion them, and let them guide you as you lead with purpose and impact. The legacy you build today through your commitment to values will echo far into the future, shaping the lives of those you lead and the organizations you build.

12
Changing the Ending.

"You can't go back and change the beginning,
but you can start where you are and change the ending."

C. S. Lewis

It is said that we have as many personalities as we have friends. Certainly, the person we are at work is often very different to who we are when we are with our closest friends. Different still to how we behave with our partner, our children, and different again with friends who are not so close. We adopt different behaviours – and with them, different values, and boundaries – with each of the different ways we show up. It is unfortunate that all the transferable skills we learn, and try to practice at work, such as people skills, effective communication, personal development, is so often left at work. Even more tragically is that our co-workers often get the best versions of us: tempered, trying, and positive, and our families get a version rude, clunky, and bordering disrespectful. We often don't recognise it at first but consider the classic 'carrot conversation' in the kitchen, for example. One of you is chopping carrots, or some other potentially controversial chore ladened with subjective rules, like loading the dishwasher, and your partner passes the un-useful comment: "that's not how you chop carrots – cut them on the diagonal!". Perhaps you might be familiar with this classic: "how many times do I need to tell you? The spoons and the knives go in the other way around!". Does it really matter? Would you have this same conversation, in the passive aggressive tone you use at home, if you were at work? Perhaps so. I'd hope not. Yet time and again I hear of difficulties, often in communication, at home. Instead of dealing with it professionally in the way we might at work; putting in more effort, implementing leadership tools and strategies, we do nothing. People skills that help us get closer to the best version of ourselves can and should be to foster stronger relationships not only with clients and colleagues but with our partners, children, friends, and families.

I grew up in a very passive aggressive household, and as such unknowingly modelled that behaviour into adulthood. It isn't a nice, kind, or effective way of communicating, but it was all I knew. It's a common white, middle class English characteristic that defines my generation and those before us, stemming from the societal norms of keeping your emotions to yourself, "being strong", and inhibiting expression. It's resulted in generations who don't know how to effectively communicate, with childhood-induced trauma that manifests as attachment, praise, and abandonment issues. It is estimated that around sixty one percent of adults have experienced at least one adverse childhood experience, with few adults recognising the impact those experiences have on our behaviours as adults. Individuals who look for recognition and validation in their work, and who need reassurance and regular praise very often experienced a lack of that in their childhoods. We seek in life the things we do not have I certainly fall into that category and don't remember much praise or validation when I was young. I'm certain it came with kindness and from a place of good intent, but my childhood was full of "see if you can do better", "try your best", and tempered praise likely intended to encourage me to be the best I can be. We didn't talk much about emotions or how we were feeling in my family, and I was encouraged, warmly and with feeling, to "stop crying"; the language clearly modelling my behaviour to not show my emotions. Differences weren't aired in our family either. If my mother was upset, you knew by how hard she slammed cupboard doors or threw things down; it was up to us to work out why and rectify it. I grew up modelling these behaviours of bottling things up, working out problems internally, and pretending as though everything was always fine, opting to walk away and not address it if it wasn't. All unhealthy behaviours but unknowingly modelled and taught to me none-the-less. And I'm not alone. In boardrooms, offices, and factory floors the world over we play out behaviours that go unchecked. Despite that, the standard of behaviour we are exhibiting at work is still more considered than that which plays out at home, with the ones we love most. It is somewhat understandable given that home is so often where we are at our most relaxed, and therefore, not trying to be anything other than who we really are. I'm not convinced that's excuse enough for making others feel less good about themselves, or for two or more people to not live in the harmony they could if each simply tried a little more.

The same strategies we employ so well at work can help us at home: seeking more knowledge and understanding before judging or acting; clear and calm communication; regular binary feedback; patience; actively building trust. Most relationships fail because of a lack of effort, and breakdown when one or both stops trying, much like in workplace culture. If the corporate focus zeros in on finding ways to consistently inspire and motivate for commercial success, that same focus should apply at home to lead with the heart for healthier and happier private spaces for relational success. We don't because we don't ask enough questions of ourselves, all too often accepting and moving blindly forwards until something traumatic jolts us alert, or we reach the end of our emotional ability to cope. Such is the human condition. But it doesn't have to be this way. Relational counselling occurs for myriad reasons, however, according to Choosing Therapy, almost fifty percent of one thousand couples sampled confirmed they had attended some form of counselling with their spouse. It is true that we hurt the ones we love, but it is also true that we simply don't try at home as much as we do at work, perhaps subconsciously prioritising employment and financial security whilst simultaneously taking for granted that those at home will always be there waiting for us when we get back.

With a few minor adjustments, almost all the strategies which work in the workplace can be applied to our home lives. For example, weekly strategy or town hall meetings at work might look at home like scheduled family time to discuss individual and family needs, plans, and to align on timing and expectations. The quarterly appraisal at work, including insightful questions as my favourite: "What happens at work that makes you want to quit?", can be a regular get-together at home with everyone sharing their favourite parts of the year as a family, and the things they found difficult with a view of resolving concerns as a family unit. Effective communication at work is what keeps everyone aligned, motivated, inspired, and wanting to do their best and this begins with active listening, feedback, and regular discussion. It shouldn't be any different at home. It can be all too easy to completely zone out after a long day, self-absorbed by the television, but when my partner began asking me over dinner: "What was your highlight of today?" it prompted active reflection, highlighted the positive aspects of the day, and an opportunity to share both of our respective experiences. Communication, connection, and a sense of value all from one simple question. I do understand that it can appear difficult on face value, putting in effort at home as well as at work, but the reality is the workplace requires much more effort than our home lives do, for arguably a less beneficial return.

It remains one of the greatest tragedies of leadership that as a craft it is still overshadowed by the oppressive, emotionally stilted ways of our predecessors who acted without care or consideration of, and with total neglect for, the person - the human being with a heart. The misogynistic and mean, the heartless and hard. The egotistical and emotionless. For too long emotional intelligence has been considered, and labelled as, a "soft skill". Somehow regarded as less important, optional, or belittled. This line of thinking is beyond ridiculous considering humans are a sentient, emotional species who feel love, fear, anxiety, anger, excitement etc. Those leaders who continue to neglect the place emotional intelligence has – or sometimes seemingly its very existence – demonstrate nothing more than a total lack of understanding of human psychology. It is tantamount to the leader of an engineering firm dismissing the importance of cogs, circuit boards, and electrical components. Respect for the 'heart' makes us better people, and in turn better leaders, because we become better at managing our core emotions – more emotionally intelligent - understanding them for ourselves, and in others. Emotional intelligence is a muscle. The more emotionally in tune we are, the better behavioural leaders we become. It's always been difficult talking about the heart space in the corporate world, and with leaders. It's been vocalised to me that it's "too soft" and "comes across a bit weak". We can dress it up in corporate jargon, if we really must, but the importance of a more human approach to leadership won't go away. I find it bewildering that people make such bold attempts to not be people; to cover up so much of what it means to be human, and to excuse that in the name of "business". It's patronising, misguided, and makes them more irrelevant as future generations become more adept at discussing how they feel, embracing individuality and expression, and including more humanistic terms and characteristics into not only conversation but their life, too.

Emotional intelligence has become something of a corporate buzz-phrase, too. But what do we really mean by it? Emotional intelligence (you'll sometimes seen it abbreviated to EI or EQ) refers to the capacity to recognize, understand, manage, and influence one's own emotions and the emotions of others. It encompasses several key components:

1. **Self-awareness**: The ability to recognize one's own emotions and how they affect thoughts and behavior.
2. **Self-regulation**: The ability to manage one's emotions and impulses effectively.
3. **Motivation**: A drive to achieve for the sake of achievement, influenced by emotional factors rather than external rewards.
4. **Empathy**: The capacity to understand and share the feelings of others, facilitating better relationships.
5. **Social skills**: Proficiency in managing relationships and building networks, fostering effective communication and conflict resolution.

Emotional intelligence is crucial in navigating social complexities, leading teams, and making informed decisions based on both rational thought and emotional insights. The term "emotional intelligence" first gained prominence in 1995, largely due to the work of psychologist Daniel Goleman. In his book, *Emotional Intelligence: Why It Can Matter More Than IQ*, Goleman synthesized earlier research and proposed that emotional intelligence is as important, if not more so, than traditional cognitive intelligence (IQ) in predicting personal and professional success.

However, it goes back further than that; the concept has roots dating back to the early twentieth century. Psychologists such as Edward Thorndike introduced the idea of "social intelligence", which included understanding and managing people. This laid the groundwork for later developments in emotional intelligence, which expanded the focus from mere social understanding to a deeper emotional awareness and regulation.

In the realm of leadership, emotional intelligence plays a critical role in effectiveness. The fact remains that leaders with high emotional intelligence are often more successful. They are adept at recognizing and interpreting emotional cues; they can tailor their messages based on the emotional state of their audience - a skill especially vital in conflict resolution, where understanding the underlying emotions can facilitate smoother negotiations.

But emotional intelligence fosters a positive work environment, too. Leaders who exhibit empathy and social skills create a culture of trust and collaboration. When team members feel understood and valued, they are more likely to contribute actively and work together effectively, and in turn this collaborative spirit enhances productivity and innovation, integrating diverse perspectives that are more likely to be respected. Being more emotionally intelligent isn't a fix-all that suddenly makes everything at work rosy. Conflict is an inevitable aspect of any workplace but leaders with high emotional intelligence are equipped to handle disagreements more constructively, more able to approach conflicts with a calm demeanor, actively listen to all parties involved, and guide discussions toward resolution. Put simply, they're more emotionally aware – in-tune. That ability to remain composed and empathetic allows them to de-escalate tensions and find mutually agreeable solutions. It also helps motivate teams through an understanding of what drives their employees, tapping into those motivations to inspire action and it is this wonderful melting point; this culmination of these behavioral elements and characteristics that underpins high performing teams because it is here, in this space where positive behaviors come together, and which often leads to higher performance and loyalty within teams.

I have spoken much here in this book and elsewhere about the importance of self-awareness in leaders and how this vulnerability, of sorts, is important to be truly emotionally intelligent. All the effective leaders I have worked with, and indeed all those interviewed for this book, are self-aware. They understand their strengths and weaknesses. This self-awareness helps regulate their emotions and reactions, especially in high-pressure situations, which is where for all humans, the cracks begin to show. Leaders who can manage their emotions are less likely to act impulsively or make decisions based on transient feelings, leading to more thoughtful and strategic decision-making. This point is important because the notion of leading from the heart, or being more emotionally aware, is often rejected for fear the exact opposite of this will be achieved.

Understanding and having proficiency in emotional intelligence is vital for leaders – it's a vastly overlooked essential characteristic, or skill. Leadership is fundamentally about relationships. It is emotional intelligence that helps us build rapport with our teams, stakeholders, and clients, and by nurturing positive relationships, we can create an atmosphere of mutual respect and cooperation, essential for achieving long-term organizational – and personal - goals.

And yet all-too-often emotional intelligence is in the "sfot skills" category. Our ability to be good at it impacts communication, team dynamics, conflict resolution, motivation, adaptability, self-regulation, and relationship-building. My hope is that more organizations recognize the importance of emotional intelligence and in turn the demand for leaders who can navigate the emotional landscape effectively will continue to grow.

In a world where technology has moved from dominating interactions to taking them over, the human element remains paramount. Those leaders who invest in developing their emotional intelligence not only enhance their effectiveness but will create healthier and more productive workplaces. As we continue to explore the nuances of emotional intelligence, it is clear that it is not just a buzzword; it is a fundamental skill set that can define the success of individuals and organizations alike.

In essence, emotional intelligence is the bridge between reason and emotion, enabling leaders to not only understand the data and dynamics of their organizations but also the hearts and minds of the people within them. As we advance into an era that values emotional connection as much as cognitive capability, cultivating emotional intelligence will undoubtedly be a cornerstone of effective leadership. Those who reject it will be left behind.

How do I begin to behave in a more emotionally intelligent way?

Perhaps this evening you will begin by saying thank you to your partner for something they have done today, or for listening or supporting you? Perhaps you will be sure to say "I love you" to your children, or spouse, and begin the process of practising appreciation and recognition more often at home. The very skills we value at work have a place in our homes. Leading from the heart doesn't have to remain a lost art.

A frequent challenge proposed to me is to resolve problematic behaviours in individuals who seemingly won't change. The history offered is usually that of an individual who just won't do as they are asked; a lone wolf in the team that is creating division and unrest among the other team players. Whoever is telling me of their challenge will likely affirm they have tried everything, to no avail. They look at me with great intrigue and anticipation, waiting for my single golden shot response to remedy the solution and immediately resolve the behaviours like a double strength migraine relief tablet. There is always something we can offer when we listen, as I always do, however, most often my answer is not what they are expecting. Leadership comes with an overbearing sense of resolution, as though the position enforces a prerequisite to resolve. However, attempting to change things of people who don't want to change is often entirely futile. We can't make people change. We can encourage, guide, model, and shape, but we can't force people to change if they do not want to. Persisting is simply a waste of energy and time – and if this resonates with your own experiences, you'll know just how much energy it takes to continually attempt to change someone. That energy and time could be better used to shape and reinforce the others in your team but knowing when to move on can be difficult, and it takes courage - one of Marshall Goldsmith's four qualities of successful leaders: courage.

The courage to lead from the heart comes from developing good feedback with your team, based on a foundation of trust and psychological safety. Feedback is supposed to be binary for it to be effective: one-way feedback is often dictatorial and accusatory. Each of us has a voice of value and purpose. We need to hear their voice, too. Everyone deserves to be seen and heard, and to feel seen and heard but they are two very different things and worth distinguishing between. We can believe we are offering those in our charge the opportunity to speak their mind, indeed we can offer an 'open-door policy', but if the intent is not supported by action, the very opposite occurs: an individual who raises a concern or offers an alternative viewpoint will silence their voice if it is met with derision, dismissal, or they are made to feel belittled. We must think carefully about which behaviours our actions help grow and flourish or quash and suppress and never let that thought leave our consciousness. The potential to change and imprint that leadership yields as the reflections in this book attest, as significant and far-reaching as any teacher.

"This too shall pass". The notion that, as my grandmother used to say, things will "blow over", is comforting. Unless you're pitching a tent. However, it's often forgotten that the phrase with its origins rooted in Persian history, also works for the good times, too. Everything will pass; good and bad. Nothing stays the same. It is a reminder of the importance of mindfulness of, and gratitude for, the present moment. Some moments we will never get back. There will come a time when we say goodbye to someone for the final time and we won't even know when that is. Of all the great leaders I have worked with, gratitude is a common characteristic among them. Gratitude for all elements of our past; for the present moment no matter how painful it is, and for the opportunity to explore a future. How much richer our working environments would be if we were all a little more grateful.

'The Leadership Legacy' isn't an actual thing, as far as I'm aware. I imagine I'm not the first person to put those three words together, but I use them to help leadership teams reflect on what they are doing with their current behaviours, the way they think, and the culture they are creating.

What will my legacy as a leader be?

When we consider how we may be remembered, and what we will leave behind, it can prompt a change in our approach. Instinctively we want to do good things. Very few people actively set out to do a bad job or to intentionally fail. If they do, they seem to settle into politics. That consciousness of legacy means finding the desire to lead with a positive influence and outcome in mind.

How can we honour those who have come before us – the leaders, teachers, and parental figures – who have positively influenced us with their legacy?

There's a great opportunity for each of us who were fortunate enough to have an especially positive leader to honor them and in turn create a positive leadership legacy of our own. It's like the ultimate act of paying it forward. How we honor that legacy I believe is a very personal choice that speaks also to our own leadership style. For example, we might publicly recognize the contributions of our mentors and role models in speeches, written tributes, or social media posts, for example. It might sound a little simplistic, but by expressing gratitude, we show appreciation for the wisdom and guidance we've received, reinforcing the importance of these influences, and simultaneously reinforcing the acts themselves in our own behaviors. The same goes whenever we share stories about the impact those mentors had on our personal and professional growth. By weaving these narratives into our leadership style, we honor those individuals and inspire others to learn from them. Witnessing this in action; this literal act of legacy in action, can be quite emotional.

In addition to simply integrating core values and principles learned from our mentors into our own leadership practices, by modeling those behaviors such as integrity, empathy, and collaboration, I have worked with leaders who went a step further establishing mentorship programs within their organizations. What a powerful way for leaders to pass on the legacy of their mentors – what a privilege! The same goes for creating awards or recognition initiatives in honor of those who have influenced them, which can simultaneously build and bond teams especially quickly when everyone in the team votes for those who have influenced them, too, for "mentor of the year", or a training or scholarship in a mentor's name, for example. In over ten years of working with leaders there isn't one who hasn't benefited from the reflective practices of journaling or regular feedback sessions that I've suggested – at least, not that they've admitted to me! In the context of legacy, these activities help shape our decisions and actions, and with those influential individuals in mind, honor their legacy in an especially human and compassionate way. Writing this reminds me of an especially inspirational lady I coached for several years, who brought her team together once a quarter for a casual meeting to discuss the influences that they each felt had shaped them, fostering an environment of appreciation, gratitude, and active self-reflection. I know we think we don't have time, but the reality is we'll always find time to do the things we wasn't to do, and as leaders we should all encourage more conversations about mentors and role models, reinforcing the importance of learning from one another. If we don't start doing leadership differently, we aren't going to get anything different.

As I come to the end of a thoroughly enjoyable time coaching the CEO of a global brand who is preparing to retire, there's one final point she prompted me to consider. It will come to a point in our careers, often with alarming suddenness, that we look to retire. We can, now, ensure our organizational values and those nostalgic lessons learned from our mentors are passed down through effective succession planning. Much like writing a will, or preparing a living will, it's one of those things many leaders never get round to. By nurturing, developing and empowering future leaders, we create a legacy that extends well beyond our tenure. It cultivates a positive legacy that inspires others, fostering a culture of growth, gratitude, and connection within our organizations.

13
Next Generation Leadership.

*"What you have learned is a mere handful;
what you haven't learned is the size of the world."*

Avaiyar

A worrying trend is the distraction of artificial intelligence (AI). Almost every conference I speak at now has at least a presentation about it with statistics, trends, and new developments, including the seemingly obligatory warning that if we don't adopt it we'll get left behind. If it's not a presentation then it's a workshop where people attempt to work out what exactly AI is and means in context to their job, all-the-while developing an underlying subtle anxiety about the possibility of losing their job to a computer. I'm not the AI expert, however, by virtue of attending more than a hundred conferences each year I've sat through more AI training than most - and I suspect probably more than some of those presenting. While there is clearly legitimacy in the consideration of AI and its role as technological advancement speeds forward like a bullet train, I do believe we've got into somewhat of a self-perpetuating frenzy. I think one lady summed it up brilliantly. Sat at the back of a conference room watching the technology expert warn about not embracing AI quickly enough before the competition did, she learnt over to me and whispered: "They've really got themselves into a tizz about this AI". We need to be careful we don't put so much focus on AI that we lose focus over the one constant consistent, and the most important aspect of almost every organisation I've worked with in the thousands over the last 21 years: people.

It is deceptively easy to get carried away with seeking solutions externally from technology and gimmicks, and indeed something I see a lot. Although it's a worrying trend, it is not only understandable but in fact entirely predictable human behaviour because of our instinctive, innate laziness; a behavioural hangover from our neolithic ancestors who understood that preserving energy and resources was critical to their survival. If someone else will do it for us, we tend to be fully embracing of it. Indeed, providers of products and services like automatic windshield wipers, or same day delivery tap into that to those who readily pay for it, nurturing our laziness and impatience. Our attractiveness to mobile apps which save us time and complete things quicker, only so we're somewhat ironically able to, in turn, do even more, plays into this very human condition. The technology of tomorrow is evermore apparently the technology of today, and the common exploration of what leading for tomorrow will look like is met with a degree of disappointment when the realisation happens that it's going to be much the same as leading for today. Our adaptation to how we incorporate, and manage, technology may well have to evolve sharply, but leadership is not about technology; it's about people. And that's where our focus as leaders needs to remain, even when unexpected and natural distractions present themselves from exciting technological advancements.

As well as technology, leadership has always also been forced to accommodate, or been the victim of, buzzwords, fads, and terminology that wane in and out of corporate fashion. Whichever is in favour at the time, many scramble to embrace and deploy in their organisations: lean working, agile working, NLP, Six Sigma, Total Quality Management, Myers-Briggs, micro learning, gamification, Matrix Management, One Minute Management, flat organisations – the list is long and at times nostalgic. The prevailing obsessions as I type this are next generation leadership, and high performance. The latter is one which regularly does the rounds, getting circled back to in similar frequency to gardening and home improvement shows on television, and I believe I know why: no one really knows what it means. I'm currently working with six clients on what could be described as high-performance training programs. Each of them first approached me to help them become a "high performing organisation" – their words. One of the first questions I ask clients at the beginning of any development journey is to describe or define what the terminology means to them. In this case: "What does the term high performance mean?". Those who had a ready answer, although four didn't, differed from the next. We appear to love the idea of self-improvement and bettering ourselves – the fact that it's estimated to be a forty billion dollar – and growing - industry certainly supports that. Being the best or high achievement is an attractive goal, especially among leaders. However, it would appear we don't quite know what it means to be that, let alone how to do it. I'm frequently asked by clients how to build high performing teams, sometimes because of my work with successful sports teams, and especially successful corporate teams, however, I suspect equally due to our innate fascination with being the best. If not owing to the toxic habit of comparison, then it comes about because of a common competitive characteristic of our species - one of the many hangovers from our primitive survival instinct that I would argue has little place in our society now. Understandably, my clients want to know how to better their teams and themselves and are often unaware that so much more can be achieved with solidarity, sharing, and compassion. Leaders don't have to be monsters to get extraordinary results.

Over the last few years, I have been analysing and working with high performing teams across several industries. One of the benefits of having global clients in varied sectors from agriculture to aerospace, pharmaceuticals to financial services, and healthcare to horticulture, is the diverse pool of talent available for me to question and because most of them know me from speaking at their company conference, or working with them on an internal training project, they are usually keen to help. If you follow me on social media, you may well have contributed to some of the public analysis we have done, and if so, thank you! Most interestingly to me is that despite the very different personality types attracted to each industry sector, with sometimes wildly different challenges, the commonality is our species: humans. The problems may be unique to the industry or the individual, but they aren't unique to our species. As such they respond with very similar answers. While my advice isn't concrete, or exhaustive, it is based on the conversations with clients, responses gathered, and many hours of discussion while analysing the behaviour traits and characteristics of individuals, teams, and organisations who others seek to emulate. Many of the high or peak performing teams produce admirably bigger or better results when compared to others in the same or similar fields. There are seven questions we can ask to help us understand and achieve high performance in ourselves and in our teams. These questions help to focus on key attributes I believe are the cornerstone of high performance.

Having said that, I'm not going to tell you what they are.

Oh, go on then.

1. "Who am I?"

Without first having a clear understanding of our identity, whether team or individual, we cannot begin to explore the other essential questions. First, we must know who we are and the intricacies of how we understand ourselves: our boundaries, like, dislikes, aspirations – it is an especially challenging question and one I'm ever-surprised people get so far in life without asking. Perhaps that is why so many reach for high performance and yearn for more? Fundamentally what is missing is not achievement but a core understanding of identity. I know from the senior leadership teams I regularly work with, and when working with organisations in crisis, there is a tendency to miss simple first steps, such as clearly defining identity, in favour of jumping ahead to what appear to be the more important, pressing problems of the moment. The answer to most problems lies outside of the problem. The result is almost always confusion and disparate connection. Take for example organisational core values, or pillars. The work begins with creating inspirational buzz words or phrases that make us feel good about working in the organisation: Customer First; Working Together; Trust. Yet no one understands how these apply to them, or the brand, or how to bring them to life because the most important foundation step is in identity. Know who you are. Only then can you create values that are clear, congruent, and relevant to you.

Begin by asking this question, then apply the same question to the team you lead ("Who are we?"), and then the wider organisation. The responses you get are worth more than any brand agency you'll pay to help you create something that sounds catchy but doesn't change performance.

2. *"Where do I/we excel?"*

We spend much time assessing our failures, but not nearly enough time considering the reasons for our successes.

What are we doing well?

Why?

How can we do it even better?

How can we move the needle more?

Be careful to maintain the focus on what you do well. With reflective exercises like this, we quickly and easily veer into the things we don't do well. From a well-being and motivation perspective, it is psychologically beneficial for us to continue moving forwards, so to speak; aiming to improve. We need to feel as though we're reaching for something that's within our grasp and progressing. Otherwise, what's the point? With no guarantee for tomorrow, and an appreciation that there were people who didn't wake up this morning, why would we settle for mediocrity, or accept average either at work or in our personal lives, when the alternative is so much more fulfilling, exciting, and purposeful?

Consider what it might look like if we focused more on what we do particularly well, spending more time displaying positive behaviours and mindsets with time dedicated to further enhancing our strengths. This is one of the foundation characteristics of all high performing teams I have worked with: acknowledgement that we all have different strengths and leaning into them as far as you can. Then surround yourselves with others who have strengths in the differing areas you are less strong. That's the basic structure of a high performing team.

3. "Who am I when no one is watching?"

This is an extension of the first question, which is almost a warm-up to this trickier question. This is one for the individual rather than a group of people. Once you have a good understanding of who you are, it's time for some deeper personal reflection.

Who are you *really*? When no one is watching and you're not having to step up to expectation, or peer pressure or to fight through a lack of confidence, or deeper insecurity, or imposter syndrome - who are you? What are your real boundaries? What do you really care about? How do you really feel about things? What are your personal ambitions, desires, and dreams? The more we shut things away, the more they eat away at us, which is precisely why so many adults are still carrying around childhood traumas or act out in ways that reveal unresolved trauma they may not even be consciously aware of. We are so expert at burying things we'd give a neurotic dog with a tasty bone a real run for its money. Instead of congruently, wholly being us we show up inauthentically in ways we feel others expect us to, and it's damaging. Gandhi preached that "the truth is always the truth", and nothing could be more fitting when it comes to the connection – or disconnection – many of us have with the real us. Knowing you, honestly and truthfully, is the only way we get to live a satisfied and fully fulfilled life. It's going to be essential for leadership in the future because generations Z and Alpha are more emotive. They willingly demonstrate and talk about how they feel and are more confident in expressing who they are.

We do not necessarily need to share the results of this very personal exercise with others, but I promise it will change how you think, feel, and ultimately behave when in situations you find conflict of self in. You don't need to be anyone else but yourself. You are enough.

4. "Why are we doing it this way?"

Many of us take comfort and solace in our habituation and comfort zones, and for obvious reason. However, a consistent characteristic of high performing teams I have worked with across sport, finance, government, and many sales teams, is the ability to regularly challenge themselves. They question whether there might be a better way of doing something, not only as part of a formal review, or a period of post-activity reflection, but at regular intervals. In workshops and meetings, I encourage the use of a timer set at random or regular intervals, either prompting everyone to pause and reflect with another question: "Why are we doing it this way?". I find it's a much more useful question when coupled with this: "How can we make it better?". As a stand-alone question, asking why we're doing things a certain way can be irritating to others, and doesn't prompt resolution or improvement, simply interrogation. The next meeting you're in, or when working in isolation on a project, set a timer to prompt you to ask these two questions. The worst outcome is reassurance that you are indeed on the right path, and should continue, but the best scenario is when you realise, entirely unintentionally, you may have drifted off course, or prompted by the question, discover an alternative way that is more beneficial.

Human behaviour isn't especially difficult to modify. It's not necessarily always easy, and certainly while it is somewhat predictable it isn't guaranteed, but it's not difficult when you know what you're doing.

5. "What culture are we actively creating?"

This question begins with a slightly different focus. Both variations of the question are important: one concerns "I", and the other "we": your wider team, or indeed entire organisation. Begin with: "What culture am I actively creating?". It's designed as a critical reflection: how are your behaviours and ways of thinking influencing the people and culture around you by virtue of how you're showing up? What is your contribution to creating a positive culture, or fulfilling cultural values, for example, through the language you choose, your outlook and attitude? Everyone in your team should consider the same, and these are, I believe, much more efficacious questions to use as part of regular reviews than some of the benign questions I've heard when sitting in on performance reviews in the past. One that particularly stands out was in an annual review (and you know how I feel about those), with a relatively despondent middle grade leader of an international bank. The review began with:

"As you know, I have to do these every year but we will keep it brief because I have a huge backlog of work and I know you've got a lot on, too." Then came this gem: "What's the one thing you've enjoyed most this year?". The individual stumbled through an answer that was about a project they contributed to, which saw them working out of the office and meeting clients. When the interview concluded and the employee left, I asked the leader what the purpose of the question was? "None really", came the reply, "I just wanted them to think positively about their time here so we can get the most out of them." There was no objective to the question; no clear value in asking it, and the answer didn't provide her with any useful information that could enhance relationship, trust, development of the individual, or even provide insight useful to develop her own leadership style and efficacy. "What culture are we actively creating?" is a single question I run entire workshop sessions on. It's deceptively simple, powerful, and helpfully reflective. In fact, the ideal question to include in appraisals and reviews, which a mutually beneficial conversation can be centred around.

The language we use matters.

6. "What does 'high performance' mean and look like for us?"

At the time of writing my team and I are working with six organisations to help them with high performance. When we begin, I ask the same question: "What does high performance mean to you?". Of those six, four didn't know. They didn't have an answer and hadn't considered it. Their answers were essentially the same: "We think it's a good thing to aspire to and we'd like to become high performing". Of the remaining two, both had different explanations of what high performance was. How can we achieve something that we are yet to define? It is at best a mystery tour road trip; the equivalent of getting in the car one day and just driving to see where you end up, reassured by the fact that you're going *somewhere.*

Defining our behaviours helps us realise them, but with a clear ultimate destination it keeps us focused through the change process, too. High performing individuals naturally struggle in environments that don't support their ability to perform and excel and so the very notion of high performing teams requires a focus on working together to achieve a common goal, using specific behaviours that everyone has been involved in developing and agreed upon. Decide what you want to see in your definition of high performing behaviours, but don't necessarily copy that from another organisation. Be inspired, and seek to emulate the success of others, if that is what reinforces or motivates you, but high performance is a very personal endeavour. What it means and looks like – not to mention how it is achieved - to Olympic winning teams, will be quite different for the country territory of a global automotive brand, for example. With an agreed upon outcome, it is infinitely easier to achieve but we can't expect behaviours that we can't name, so while this may seem an overly simplistic and unremarkable question to ask, it creates a baseline and tangible objective for all. It can help define your purpose while serving as a perpetual reminder to keep you on track. Without answering it, you don't have a defined outcome, identified destination or objective.

7. "What legacy am I leaving?"

In 2017 I began writing a book about legacy. The book remains unfinished, as does my thinking on it. The two are probably interlinked. This last week I was speaking to a client and as we got to the end of the call, he said: *"I just want to say something before we finish. You said something when we spoke last time that's been on my mind since. I commented on your lovely bookcase behind you and said you must be doing well for yourself, to which you replied: 'I know my worth'. I've been thinking about that ever since because I don't think I know my worth. I don't think I've ever considered it before."* My client isn't alone. In the research I did for the book about legacy, I struggled to find many people who had contemplated the legacy they are leaving, and almost none were consciously working to leave one. A common question posed when we consider our worth, or the value we bring to our role or organisation is: "If you didn't turn up to work for a week, or a month, would the organisation survive without you? If it would, then perhaps you need to consider the true value you bring." The question itself is a little trite, and subject to legitimate challenge. I'm unaware of any role that isn't replaceable. During times of crisis, we step up; we enhance team collaboration; we adapt and evolve as individuals, teams, and organisations. Nothing lasts forever and so we must be able to replace and move forwards. However, within the question there is an important context. What value or worth do you bring to your role? With a global population of almost eight billion people, it's unrealistic to believe there isn't *someone* who could step into your shoes and do what you do at least close to the way you do it – or better. Without an understanding of our true value, we underperform, which in turn leads to job dissatisfaction. There exists a fine line between knowing you are good at something, and arrogance. It's a line we must carefully navigate like a tightrope walker increasing the rope's distance from the ground below. But with practice we get better if we consistently practice self-awareness -a skill hugely under-developed in leadership.

The right questions to ask are often the simplest ones you don't think to ask. However, the right questions are also often the most profound. "What legacy am I leaving?" is one such question many have not asked themselves. It's a powerful question for a parent to ask, making us aware of the importance of the decisions and choices we make that influence our children, their behaviour and future. As leaders though, it is a fundamental question that helps with self-awareness, and one I encourage all who I work with to ask themselves regularly as part of quarterly reflection. Our legacy is as much about our intent, as it is deepening our understanding of what we are doing and why we are doing it for an ultimate sense of achievement and realisation. Some projects are never finished; some jobs never complete; some causes unresolved, however, a clear intention of what we are working or fighting for is essential. If we are here only once, we owe it to ourselves if no one else to fully understand why we do the things we do. What do we hope to achieve and how? What do we want to leave behind? How can we leave our teams, organisations, part of the world, communities, families, better for our having been here? Otherwise, what is the point? What are you doing this for, if not for something greater?

It is understandable that so few have contemplated the simple yet powerful question: "What legacy am I leaving?" given the workloads and pressures I witness leaders are having to navigate. We don't need more deadlines, or workload, or targets. What we need is more time. The greatest gift we can give ourselves is time. Time to pause. Time to reflect and recover. To be present and active in our thinking to ask and answer more questions that challenge us and our collective way of working; the decisions we make, and to be aware of the support our bodies and minds need. The workload will continue to relentlessly pile up unless we do something differently. The model of leadership that is widespread employed is fundamentally broken. Working into the long hours with the aim to reduce or eliminate a burgeoning to-do list is futile and misguided – and the rejection of self-awareness I witness, in favour of getting the list done, is damaging beyond what we are aware. We won't willingly touch a hot iron because the positive punishment feedback is immediate. We wouldn't expect our laptops to function continuously without the need for charging, or software updates, or even the occasional shut down or reset, but these are mere machines not even a fraction of the complexity and potential of you, a human. The dramatic result of burnout or overwhelm is longer periods of down time managing sickness, whether physical or emotional, that result in more dramatic, long-term consequences.

Why are we doing that to ourselves, and to those in our team?

Why do we continue to exhibit the same behaviours, yet expect different results?

Why do we ignore prioritising regular, well-managed rest and recuperation periods – or simply better management of our time?

These aren't rhetorical, but questions I'd encourage you to stop and consider now.

What isn't working, and why isn't it working?

What is within our power to change?

Who do we need to help us achieve it?

The cornerstone of high performance, and of all effective teams I have had the immense pleasure of working with thus far, is self-awareness. It is time we gave ourselves more time.

Final Thoughts.

"The greatest danger to our future is apathy."

Jane Goodall

This is the first time I've put my thoughts about, and the systems I use to teach leadership, into print. I sincerely hope they serve you well both in practice and in the way you frame and think about leadership, and that you see the value of them for your personal life, too.

I have for many years practised Buddhism, and my relationship with it is perhaps a little more practical for those of us not living in a monastery or Buddhist community like Plum Village in France. Incidentally, the founder of Plum Village, the great Buddhist Zen Master Thích Nhât Hanh, was influential in making Buddhism relevant for the modern world, and it is he and the Plum Village Tradition that has influenced my own practice. It was clear to me that key principles in Buddhism could be hugely useful for helping resolve common challenges in leadership, both as a craft and as a position. Our reality is that we live in a world we are rarely present for. It is one of the tragic observations I make in my role as a behaviourist: people living their lives as if it is a bizarre rehearsal, and that one day they'll get to do it all over again with all the mistakes and imperfect parts removed. Buddhism introduced us to mindfulness as a core part of its practice. Mindfulness as a concept brings us to a singular moment: this very moment, right now, as you read this. You are, right now, as you follow these words, for as long as you're only concentrating on these words without thinking about anything else, practising mindfulness to a degree. It is that strikingly simple. Practicing mindfulness helps us recognise the simplicity of life: you breathe in and as you do so are mindful of that inward breath. You then breathe out and are wholly focused on that outward breath. If you do it correctly, focused only on the action and feeling of drawing a breath in, and then releasing an outward breath, it's not possible to be aware of anything else but your breath. A state of total mindfulness. Its power is not solely in calming us down, but in helping us be very much in the present moment. When we are more capable of being in the present moment, it radically changes our ability to manage the impact external factors have on us. We can live more fully and mindfully. One small tool used in this way can be so beneficial when contemplating the right decision to make; when considering a challenge; before reacting to a triggering email or comment, or when we are aware of external factors having a negative impact on how we feel. We can simply breathe.

When I talk about the importance of humanity in leadership, I think of the practical and useful Buddhist principles I have been using with leaders over the last two decades, and teaching audiences to apply in the context of personal and professional development. The synergy is too useful to ignore.

Being present in each moment is at the core of all Buddhist teaching. This moment, right now as you read this, is the only one we can control, and in terms of regulating our response and what we allow to impact us, the only one that matters. It has become a toxic human trait to worry about things that have already happened and which we no longer have any control of, going over interactions over and over in our mind: "I should have said..."; "I wish I hadn't...?"; "It makes me so angry to think...". It isn't just the past we worry about though; we give so much energy and attention to the very things that haven't happened yet, too! We play and replay out the various possible scenarios, variations, possible outcomes, and approaches, all the while missing the opportunity to be present now. It is a habit I see in many who have high-pressured positions. The triggering of the autoimmune system by ever-present stress elevates adrenaline and cortisol levels that make it physiologically challenging to be present with control. Instead, they fiddle with their pen, or constantly rearrange things on their desk, jiggle their leg, tense their jaw, dart their eyes around a room. These energy-driven behaviours are fallout of the rising levels of stress hormones that have no other outlet. When those stress levels are especially high, it is extremely difficult to be still and calm. Only with conscious calming and deeper breathing to lower our heart rate and regain control, are we able to be present again. The challenge for those who are not present is that they do not know. The displacement behaviours of pen-tapping, nail-biting, and frenetic behaviour are not conscious; they are driven by rising stress hormones and the associated biological chemistry. Being present, however, is a conscious choice. To be ever mindful, or at least regularly mindful, of why we are doing what we are doing is how we are able to notice when we are not.

I believe leadership as a field of learning that models human behaviour and has the legacy for great change, and as a craft, has lost its way. A person-centred approach is how I believe we improve what leaders can do, and the impact they can have. To truly understand the concept of people leading people means we must first be vulnerable to better understanding ourselves.

One of the teachings of the Plum Village Tradition of Buddhism is to call what we feel by its name: to identify precisely what we feel to better understand why so we can navigate it safely, and more importantly understand what to do about it. For example, it may be that a particular emotional response or reflection on how you behaved sees you identifying your ego, or that you identify what you feel as fear, vulnerability, anxiety, anger etc. We all innately know what guilt feels like: when we experience it, we don't verbalise it that way though. We don't need to because we've experienced guilt before, learnt how it manifests, and instantly recognise the emotion. It's the same for almost all emotions. We don't find ourselves feeling jealous and say: "Oh, I know that feeling; I'm feeling jealous!" - we simply know and understand the emotion instinctively, without having to name it. However, by naming it, the way the emotion is processed changes; it no longer becomes an entirely emotive experience but a cerebral one. We can consciously unpick how we got there:

Why am I feeling [jealousy]?

What has triggered that feeling?

Why did I get [jealous]?

Does that remind me of something that happened before in my life that I was uncomfortable with?

We can't deal with emotions we can't name.

One of the teachings of Zen Master Thích Nhât Hanh is a cautionary tale of eating rotten apples. The warning is of eating a rotten apple, lest we become unwell. The apple is a metaphor for being mindful of what we consume because what we consume, we become. How I feel when stood in a night club at midnight listening to a DJ playing loud party music is very different to how I might feel when sat in a quiet woodland listening to the gentle rustle of trees in the breeze. The language we use about ourselves ("I'm fat", "I'm too skinny", "I'm fine") creates our story. Surround ourselves with negativity in the books we read, the television we watch, and the people we socialise with, and our own outlook in turn becomes more negative. Conversely, listening to positive topic podcasts, inspiring books, and supportive people helps us have a more resilient, optimistic, and balanced outlook on life. The challenge leaders face is to acknowledge and handle negative aspects of people, circumstance, and environment whilst not consuming them. It can be all too easy to become a part of the problem by allowing external aspects to influence how we think, feel, or behave - but choosing what we let impact us remains our greatest human freedom.

There's plenty we can do to become more self-aware, and to intentionally choose right behaviors. We are of course allowed to make mistakes; it is what we do about them that people care about most. For example, many people are not good listeners. They are too distracted by what they want their contribution to be, or what they are going to say and so they don't hear what is being said. I recently met the TED talk phenomenon that is Julian Treasure. His talks have attracted millions of views from people interested in listening to his thoughts on listening effectively and speaking effectively. It is perhaps telling that his presentation on speaking effectively has been viewed more than his one about listening. We like to talk more than we care to listen. The focus is so often selfishly on us, as if we are more important than the other person, perhaps best demonstrated by the ultimate in distracted people: the ones who frequently look over your shoulder as you are talking to them, visually searching the room. Or the person who asks you a question and cuts you off mid answer to ask something else or add their own contribution. Whilst these behaviours are common in those with attention deficit disorders or autism, they are also prevalent in the perpetually distracted; those with an unquiet mind. While it can understandably be interpreted as rudeness, what it really reveals is the level at which they are distracted and their ultimate lack of presence.

I have a timer on my iPhone, a gentle bell, that chimes every forty-five minutes. Its purpose is to bring me back to the present moment and there isn't a single time it goes off when I am ready for it, or my attention not entirely wrapped in something. It is remarkable how quickly we become absorbed by the myriad distractions offered to us daily. On the chime, I momentarily stop what I am doing and bring my attention to my breath, being conscious of simply breathing in and out for a few moments. It is practical mindfulness that offers me an opportunity to pause, reset, and check just how far I've drifted from my intention of being calm and present. If nothing else this sort of regular technique helps to develop positive new habits providing opportunity to self-check that we haven't drifted too far off course:

How am I presenting myself?

Am I the best version of myself right now?

In Tibetan Buddhism the known gap between where we desire or hope to be and the space where one feels lost and without direction, where old habits no longer apply and we struggle through change, is called a bardo. It's a lonely and confusing space to be, however, it is also a place of great transformation. A key lesson in Buddhism is to trust the process; to understand that the journey is the destination. There is no ultimate end place because the environment is us, and that end goal is always replaced by another if that's all we ever seek. There's too much change happening all the time, and too many parameters which impact our journey to arrive at a singular space or objective where everything is sorted or figured out. And yet we often fool ourselves that when this week is over, or when this piece of work is done, everything will be okay. That idea is less like herding cats, as the phrase goes, and more akin to herding an ant colony, if each ant was a moving part of our lives. So it is with leadership, too. It is never finished. It is a craft that we hone and develop over time, continuously. It is worth living in the present for, to be evermore aware of what requires our attention and focus. Many of the people I have coached or worked with who are leaders are in the equivalent of something of a leadership bardo. To lead in a human-centred way, in which we better understand, appreciate, and value human behavior, is to move away from that strange place.

What would happen if I trusted the process more, in the present moment, instead of attempting to look and live into the future where none of those things are guaranteed?

We need to get back to discovering who we really are, to support each other to live honestly and more compassionately for the health of our body and mind, and for the future of effective leadership.

As leaders, we must find the courage to lead authentically, wholly, and with purpose. I hope, in turn, you discover the best version of you and can help lead others to do the same.

What will you do to do it different?

Jez Rose, England, 2024

References.

What Makes Leadership Development Programs Succeed?: Hbr.org. Pub. Dec. 4, 2023, https://hbr.org/2023/02/what-makes-leadership-development-programs-succeed#:~:text=Every%20year%2C%20global%20organizations%20spend,teams%20are%20not%20always%20clear.

Applying Behavioural Insight to Organ Donation: https://assets.publishing.service.gov.uk/government/uploads/system/uploads/attachment_data/file/267100/Applying_Behavioural_Insights_to_Organ_Donation.pdf

Leadership Statistics:
Zippia. "36 Powerful Leadership Statistics [2023]: Things All Aspiring Leaders Should Know" Zippia.com. Pub. Feb. 9, 2023, https://www.zippia.com/advice/leadership-statistics/

Childhood Trauma and Its Effect on Adulthood:
Palo Alto University. Pub. Dec, 13, 2023, https://concept.paloaltou.edu/resources/business-of-practice-blog/childhood-trauma#:~:text=Approximately%2061%25%20of%20adults%20have,or%20more%20adverse%20childhood%20experiences.

Marriage Counselling:
Choosingtherapy.com Pub. Dec. 21, 2023, https://www.choosingtherapy.com/marriage-counseling-statistics/#:~:text=General%20Couples%20Therapy%20Stats,of%20counseling%20with%20their%20spouse.&text=Couples%20go%20to%20therapy%20for,issues%20to%20healing%20after%20infidelity.

Global Self Improvement Market Worth:

Globenewswire.com Pub. Nov. 30, 2023,
https://www.globenewswire.com/en/news-release/2023/11/30/2788922/0/en/Latest-Global-Self-Improvement-Market-Size-Share-Worth-USD-81-6-Billion-by-2032-at-a-8-CAGR-Custom-Market-Insights-Analysis-Outlook-Leaders-Report-Trends-Forecast-Segmentation-Grow.html#:~:text=%E2%80%9CAccording%20to%20the%20latest%20research,growth%20rate%20(CAGR)%20of%20about

"Pauline Clance The psychologist who first identified imposter syndrome no longer feels it".
Financial Times magazine. Pub. Feb. 10, 2024

Printed in Great Britain
by Amazon

51968313R00092